Talking About Japan-Q&A

装幀●菊地信義
装画●野村俊夫

執筆●井上恵一
小沢絵里子
佐近忠弘
保坂美枝

翻訳●Patricia Mari Katayama
Hisako Nozaki Ifshin
Kirsten Rochelle McIvor
Babel International

編集●翻訳情報センター

Published by Kodansha International Ltd.,
17-14, Otowa 1-chome, Bunkyo-ku, Tokyo 112-8652.

First Edition 1996

ISBN4-7700-2026-0
98 99 00 01 02 25 24 23 22 21 20 19

英語で話す「日本」Q&A
Talking About Japan–Q&A

講談社インターナショナル［編］

まえがき

新しく創刊されたバイリンガル・ブックス・シリーズの第一巻として、本書をお届けいたします。講談社インターナショナルは、30年以上にわたって日本の文化を海外に紹介する仕事を続けてまいりましたが、今はインターネットに象徴されるように、各国の文化が国境をかるがると越えて交流する時代です。わたくしたちに課せられた使命にもおのずと新しいテーマが加わってきました。

その一つが日本人のバイリンガル化に対応する出版です。国際交流のツールとしての言語が英語である以上、日本人も英語を修得せざるを得ません。これは容易なことではありませんが、どうしても乗り越えなければならない壁です。そこへのワン・ステップとして、日本語でも英語でも自分の読みたい言語で本が読める、そして自由に切り替えられる—こういうことを考えてバイリンガル・ブックスを発刊いたしました。小社が今まで培ってきた英語出版と文化紹介のノーハウを駆使して、新しいテーマの本を続々とお届けいたします。また外国の人がこのシリーズを直接読むことによって、日本語の勉強になったり、日本に対する理解が促進されることも期待しています。

第一巻は国際交流の基礎である、日本のすべてを説明する本です。外国の人と交際するときに、これだけは知っておきたい日本に関する知識を、できるかぎり面白く、やさしい英語で話せるようにしてあります。いろいろな場で皆様のお役に立つことを願ってやみません。

講談社インターナショナル株式会社

Preface

This book is the first volume in our new Bilingual Books Series. For over thirty years, Kodansha International has engaged in the task of introducing Japanese culture to foreign readers. But as epitomized today by the Internet, this is an age when all nations can effortlessly cross borders and engage in culture exchange. New tasks have found their way into our entrusted mission.

One of these is to encourage the "bilingual-ization" of the Japanese. As long as English remains the main vehicle for international exchange, Japanese must master this language. Although this is no simple undertaking, it is nevertheless a hurdle we must overcome. As one step toward this goal, what we felt was needed was a book that could be read in either English or Japanese, a book that would allow us to switch back and forth as we pleased—and with this concept in mind, we created the Bilingual Books Series. Making most of all the know-how on cultural exchange and English-language publishing that we have gained over the years, we will present you with a continuous selection of new titles with new themes. We also welcome foreign readers to this series, and hope that our books will serve to further their Japanese language skills and deepen their understanding of Japan.

This first volume will introduce all aspects of Japan and serve as a primer for international exchange. It is designed to help you explain, clearly and in an engaging manner, all the essential information you need to know about Japan for your next encounters with English-speaking friends. We sincerely hope this volume will prove to be useful to you in a variety of situations.

Kodansha International Ltd.

目次

1. 日本の国土と自然

日本の国土

日本の地形

日本の気候

日本の自然災害

Contents

2. 日本のルーツと歴史

日本の誕生

日本の国歌・国旗

日本語

日本の天皇

2. ORIGIN AND HISTORY OF JAPAN

Birth of Japan

Japan's National Anthem and National Flag

Japanese Language

The Emperor of Japan

Japanese History

From Meiji to the Present

3. GOVERNMENT AND ECONOMY

Constitution of Japan

Government System

経済・産業・貿易

日本の税金

日本の警察と犯罪

Economy, Industry and Trade

Taxes in Japan

Police System and Crimes in Japan

日本の防衛

4. 日本の社会

日本の人口と家族

日本人の特質

日本の教育

The Defense System of Japan

4. JAPANESE WAY OF LIFE AND SOCIETY

Japan's Population and Families

The Characteristics of the Japanese

Education in Japan

日本人と仕事

年金

日本の医療

日本の宗教

The Japanese at Work

Pensions and Insurances

Medicine in Japan

Religions in Japan

5. 日本の文化

現代の文化

日本の伝統的な文化

5. CULTURE

Comtemporary Culture

Traditional Culture of Japan

6. 日本人の衣食住

日本人の衣生活

日本人の食生活

日本人の住生活

6. CLOTHING, CULINARY LIFE AND HOUSING IN JAPAN

Clothing of the Japanese

Culinary Life of the Japanese

Housing in Japan

7. 生活と習慣

日本の祝休日・祭り

日本の結婚

日本の葬式

7. LIFE AND CUSTOMS

Japanese Holidays and Festivals

Japanese Marriages

Funerals in Japan

日本人の余暇・娯楽

日本のスポーツ

日常の生活・習慣

Leisure Time and Recreation of the Japanese

Sports in Japan

Daily Life in Japan

1

日本の国土と自然

日本の国土

Q: 日本は地球上のどこにあるのですか？

中央に日本がある世界地図を想像してみてください。どの国でも，自分の国を地図の中心に据えています。日本の地図もそうです。

そこで，あなたがヨーロッパ人なら，日本を英語でFar East「極東」と称したように，イタリア半島の南端からアテネを経て，北緯36度に沿って東へ東へと進み，アジア大陸のイラン北部から中国大陸を横断し，そのはずれの海を渡れば日本列島の中央部にたどりつくと考えてください。

アメリカ人なら，サンフランシスコから太平洋を真西に進めば日本の東京にたどりつきます。緯度からすれば，ニューヨークは本州の北端の青森県，パリは北海道の北部にあたりますし，ロンドンは日本の北端よりも上の緯度の位置になります。

1

LAND AND NATURE OF JAPAN

Land of Japan

• Where on the earth is Japan located?

Imagine a world map with Japan in the center. In any country people make maps with their own country in the middle of the map, and so is the case with the Japanese.

If you are in Europe, you call Japan the "Far East," and think of its location this way: you get there by heading toward the east starting from the southern end of the Italian Peninsula. You go through Athens, continue to make your way east along the 36 degree north latitude to Iran and then you traverse the Asian Continent across China, and cross the Sea of Japan, which will take you to the center of the Japanese Islands.

If you are in America, keep going west from San Francisco, and you will eventually reach Tōkyō. New York is situated on the same latitude as Aomori Prefecture, the northern part of Honshū (main island) of Japan. Paris is on the same latitude as the northern part of Hokkaidō, and London is located north of the northernmost tip of Japan.

Q: 日本の大きさはどれくらいですか？

日本の陸地の面積は約378,000km²です。日本は小さい国とよく言われますが，それでも，日本の北から南のはてまでとなると，約3,500kmはあり，その風景の変化たるや他の国とは違った多彩な姿を持っています。

しかし実を言うと，アメリカの州の1つであるカリフォルニア州よりも日本が小さいということは，あまり知られていません。カリフォルニア州は約411,000km²もあります。

Q: 日本の現在の領土はいつ決まったのですか？

1945年，日本は第2次世界大戦の敗戦国となり，この時点で，日清戦争（1894年）以前の領土に縮小させられ，現在は，北海道，本州，四

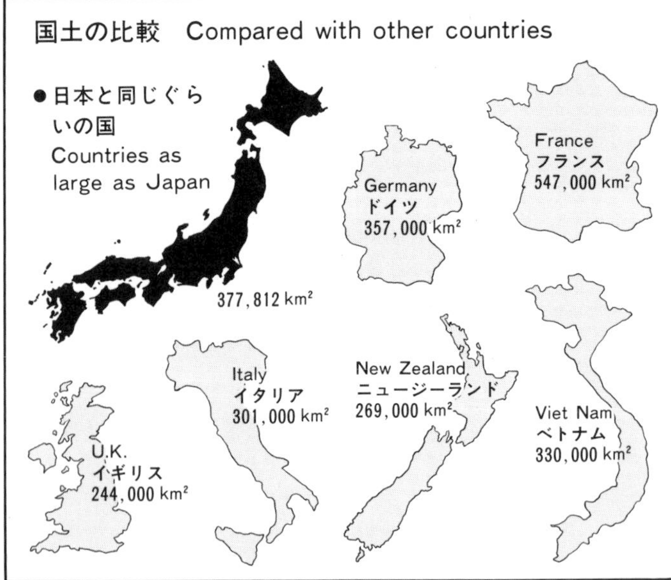

• How big is Japan?

Japan's land area is approximately 378,000 km². It is often said that Japan is a small country. However, the archipelago stretches some 3,500 km from the northernmost end to the southernmost end, which means that climate and scenery vary greatly from region to region.

A fact that is not very well known is that Japan is smaller than California in the United States, which has a land area of about 411,000 km².

• When was Japan's present territory determined?

In 1945, when Japan was defeated in World War II, its land was reduced to its present size prior to the Sino-Japanese War in 1894. Today Japan consists of four main islands:

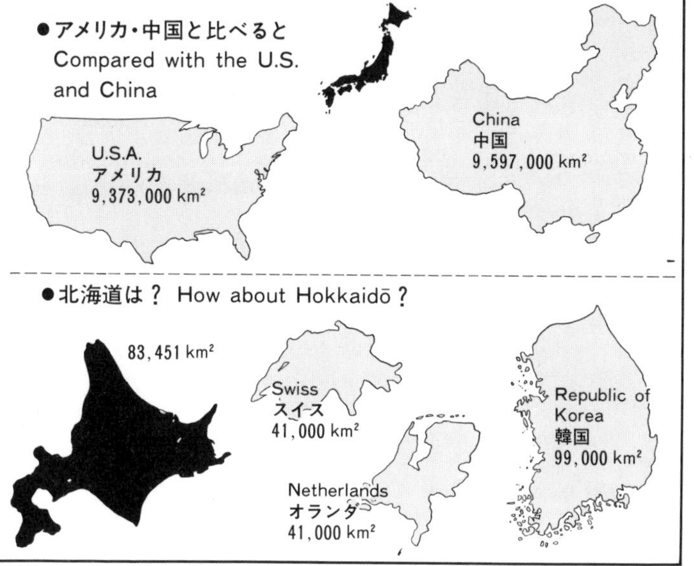

国，九州，沖縄と数千の小さな島々で成り立っています。

沖縄は，1951年のサンフランシスコ講和条約締結後も，そのままアメリカの施政権下に置かれ，日本に復帰したのは1972年でした。

終戦までに日本が領土としていたのは，現在の領土のほかに，樺太，千島列島，韓国，台湾がありますが，世界の目からは，日本が「侵略」して保有したと解釈されました。

現在，千島列島の南部の歯舞(はぼまい)島，色丹(しこたん)島，国後(くなしり)島，択捉(えとろふ)島は日本固有の領土であるという主張のもとに，ロシアとの交渉が行われています。

沖縄県の八重山諸島の北，約160kmのところにある小島群の尖閣(せんかく)諸島は，沖縄県の石垣市に属していますが，中国と台湾が領土権を主張して問題になっています。

Q:沖縄も昔から日本だったのですか?

明治維新（1868年）の時はまだ，沖縄は日本ではなかったのです。沖縄の旧名の「琉球」というのは中国人による命名で，15世紀初期から，琉球王国という1つの国として存在していました。しかし，国としての力は弱く，当時の中国の清国と，日本の薩摩藩の両方に従属した形で存続を保っていました。

Okinawan dance

1872年に政府は琉球国王を琉球藩王として，日本に組み込もうとします。そして，当時の清国からの抗議がないまま，1879年になると，日本政府は琉球を沖縄県にしてしまいました。

沖縄に行くと，風土は日本でもあり，中国でもあり，また東南アジアでもあり，という感じがし

Hokkaidō, Honshū, Shikoku, and Kyūshū, plus the Okinawa Islands, and thousands of other smaller islands.

Okinawa remained under American control even after the San Francisco Peace Treaty in 1951, when it was returned to Japan in 1972.

Until the end of World War II, Japan owned Sakhalin, the Kuril Islands, Korea and Taiwan, which was regarded by the rest of the world as taken by Japan by aggression.

Currently, Japan claims the southern part of the Kuril Islands including the Habomai Islands, Shikotan, Kunashiri, and Etorofu as part of its territory, and negotiations with Russia are an ongoing issue.

Another area in dispute is the Senkaku Islands, which is under the jurisdiction of Ishigaki city, 160 km north of the Yaeyama Islands in Okinawa Prefecture, for which not only Japan but also China and Taiwan claim territorial rights.

• Has Okinawa been a part of Japan from ancient times?

Okinawa was not a part of Japanese territory at the time of the Meiji Restoration (1868), the dawn of the modernization of Japan. Okinawa's former name, Ryūkyū, was given by the Chinese. The Ryūkyū Kingdom existed from the beginning of the 15th century, but since it was a weak country, it sought support from both the Ching Dynasty of China and the Satsuma Clan of Japan.

In 1872, the Japanese government tried to incorporate Ryūkyū into Japan and in 1879 changed its name to Okinawa Prefecture without any protest from the Ching government.

Visitors may have the impression that Okinawa is both physically and spiritually a mixture of Japan, China and

ます。しかし，琉球方言と言われる沖縄の言葉は，他の日本語の方言と異なって聞こえますが，同じ日本語であると考えられています。

日本の地形

Q: 日本はどんな地形をしていますか？

日本は「山国」と言うことができます。アメリカのカリフォルニア州よりも小さいのに，日本の67%は山地で，平野はわずか13%しかありません。

その山地から流れ出る多くの川が，日本各地に大小の谷を作り，地形に様々な変化を与えています。そして河口に扇形の堆積平野を作っていますが，関東平野，大阪平野，濃尾平野などいくつかを除いて，いずれも狭い平野です。

日本の海岸線は非常に長く，その延長は約34,000kmあり，複雑な海岸線が，地域から地域へと移り変わる風景美を見せています。

Byōbugaura

Q: 日本に島はいくつありますか。その中でいちばん大きい島は？

日本はおよそ6,800の島で成り立っています。その中には，人も住まないような島もあります。

面積が大きいほうから並べれば，国後（くなしり）島、択捉（えとろふ）島を除いて大きい島は，本州，北海道，九州，四国，そして沖縄の5つということになりますが，実は，日本人が“島”というときにはこの5つは含みません。“島”と呼ぶのは，これ以外のもっと小さな“島”なのです。

その中で最大の島と言うと，本州中央部の北，日本海に浮かぶ佐渡島ということになりま

Southeast Asia. The language, however, called the Ryūkyū dialect, is considered to be similar to the Japanese language, although it sounds different from the other dialects.

Geography of Japan

• What is the geography of Japan like?

Japan can be described as a mountainous country. Although it is a little smaller than California. Sixty seven percent of its entire land surface is covered with mountains, and plains account for only 13%.

Rivers running from the mountains carve numerous valleys and gorges, and give a great deal of variety to the country's topographical features. At the mouths of rivers, fan-shaped deltas are formed, most of which are very small except for the Kantō Plain, Ōsaka Plain, and Nōbi Plain.

The coast lines of this island nation are extremely long, stretching for nearly 34,000 km. The complicated coastal line of Japan is indicative of the scenic beauty that varies from region to region.

• How many islands are there in Japan and which one is the largest?

Japan is made up of about 6,800 islands, some of which are not inhabited.

The five largest islands excluding Kunashiri and Etorofu are Honshū, Hokkaidō, Kyūshū, Shikoku and Okinawa, in descending order. In fact, these five islands are not usually included in what the Japanese refer to as "islands." When they say islands, they mean much smaller isles scattered around the main islands.

The largest of these isles is Sado Island, located north of central Honshū, lying in the Sea of Japan. Its land area is about

す。面積は約857km²，周囲約217kmあります。

Q: 日本の湖はいくつありますか。その中でいちばん大きい湖は？

Lake Biwa

実に多くの湖があり正確な数ははっきりしませんが，面積が1km²以上の湖沼は100ぐらいあります。その中で最大の湖は琵琶湖です。

この琵琶湖は世界的に有数の古い淡水湖です。約500万年前に今の三重県あたりで誕生し，地殻変動で北へ動き，現在の滋賀県の位置に達したのは，約120万年前だと言われています。

面積は約673km²ですが，世界の淡水湖のスペリオル湖の82,360km²，ヒューロン湖の59,570km²などに比べれば，けた違いに小さな湖です。

主な日本の山・川・湖・島
Main mountains, rivers, lakes and islands in Japan

■山　Five Major Mountains

山の名(Name)		所在地(Location)	高さ(Height)
富士山	Fuji-san	Yamanashi, Shizuoka	3,776 m
北岳	Kita-dake	Yamanashi	3,192 m
奥穂高岳	Okuhotaka-dake	Nagano, Gifu	3,190 m
間ノ岳	Aino-take	Yamanashi, Shizuoka	3,189 m
槍ヶ岳	Yariga-take	Nagano	3,180 m

■川　Five Major Rivers

川の名(Name)		所在地(Location)	長さ(Length)
信濃川	Shinano-gawa	Nagano, Niigata	367 km
利根川	Tone-gawa	Gumma, Ibaraki, Chiba, etc.	322 km
石狩川	Ishikari-gawa	Hokkaidō	268 km
天塩川	Teshio-gawa	Hokkaidō	256 km
北上川	Kitakami-gawa	Iwate, Miyagi	249 km

857 km^2 and its circumference is about 217 km.

- **How many lakes are there in Japan? Which one is the largest?**

It is hard to tell the exact number, but as far as lakes larger than 1 km^2 are concerned, there are about 100 across the nation. The largest lake is Lake Biwa.

Lake Biwa is one of the oldest freshwater lakes in the world. It is believed that this lake dates back 5 million years ago. It moved north from its original location in Mie Prefecture to Shiga Prefecture because of diastrophism or crust movement that occurred 1.2 million years ago.

The area of the lake is about 673 km^2, which is far smaller than some of the larger lakes in the world such as Lake Superior (82,360 km^2) and Lake Huron (59,570 km^2).

■湖　Five Major Lakes

湖の名前(Name)		所在地(Location)	面積(Area)
琵琶湖	Biwa-ko	Shiga	672 km^2
霞ヶ浦	Kasumiga-ura	Ibaraki	168 km^2
サロマ湖	Saroma-ko	Hokkaidō	152 km^2
猪苗代湖	Inawashiro-ko	Fukushima	104 km^2
中海	Nakaumi	Tottori, Shimane	98 km^2

■島　Five Major Islands

島の名前(Name)		所在地(Location)	面積(Area)
択捉島	Etorofu-tō	Hokkaidō	3,139 km^2
国後島	Kunashiri-tō	Hokkaidō	1,500 km^2
沖縄島	Okinawa-jima	Okinawa	1,185 km^2
佐渡島	Sadoga-shima	Niigata	857 km^2
奄美大島	Amami-ōshima	Kagoshima	709 km^2

Q: 日本でいちばん高い山は？

もちろん富士山です。高さは3,776mで，チョモランマの8,848mをはじめとする世界の高峰から見れば，大したことはありません。しかし，平地から三角形にそびえ立つ姿の美しさは日本を代表する景観です。

この休火山の頂上には，直径が800m，深さ200mの火口があります。古くから霊山として信仰の対象となっている山で，その端正な姿は多くの俳句，短歌によまれています。

多くの有名な画家が富士山の絵に挑戦していますが，その中でも，江戸時代の浮世絵師，葛飾北斎が，富士山をいろいろな角度から，いろいろな時間，季節の中で描いた「富嶽三十六景」は特に有名です。

Q: 日本には火山はいくつありますか？

Mt. Fugen

日本には80くらいの活火山があります。世界の活火山800ほどのうち，約10％が日本に集中していることになります。その日本には，北から南まで7つの火山帯が走っており，それぞれがいくつかの活発な火山を抱えているのです。

近年の最大の爆発は長崎県島原の雲仙・普賢岳(ふげんだけ)の噴火です。1990年に約200年ぶりに噴火し，火砕流によって43人もの命が失われ，島原市の一部が溶岩で覆われ，多数の人が避難生活を送りました。

• What is the highest mountain in Japan?

It is the famous Mt. Fuji which is 3,776 meters high. It cannot in no way be compared with the world's highest peaks such as Mt. Everest (Chomolungma, 8,848 meters) in terms of height. However, it has become emblematic of Japan with the striking beauty of its nearly perfect conical profile and wide-flowing skirts.

At the peak of this dormant volcano, there is a crater, 800 meters across and 200 meters deep. From ancient times, Mt. Fuji has been an object of worship as a sacred mountain, and its perfection has long been celebrated in traditional verses such as *haiku* and *tanka*.

Many renowned artists have taken up the challenge to depict Mt. Fuji in pictures. Among them, Katsushika Hokusai, an ukiyo-e woodblock print artist in the Edo period (1603–1867), won great acclaim in his *Fugaku Sanjū-rokkei* (36 scenes of Mt. Fuji), in which he painted Mt. Fuji from various perspectives, at various hours of the day, in each season.

• How many volcanoes are there in Japan?

There are about 80 active volcanoes. It is said that about 10% of the 800 world's active volcanoes are concentrated in Japan. Seven volcanic belts run across the country, each of which has several active volcanoes.

One of the recent major eruptions was that of Mt. Fugen in Shimabara, Nagasaki Prefecture. This volcano erupted in 1990 for the first time in 200 years. Its pyroclastic flow killed 43 people and lava discharged from its crater covered part of Shimabara city. Many people were forced to evacuate from their homes.

Q: 富士山は今度はいつ噴火しそうですか？

Mt. Fuji

残された最初の記録によれば，富士山は，781年を最初として，1083年までに13回，約30年ごとに噴火を繰り返していました。

ところが，その次の14回目の爆発までは，428年間も間があき，1511年から1707年の間に3回噴火があっただけです。火山活動は観測されておらず，富士山は休眠中です。しかし，富士山も噴火の可能性がゼロということではないそうです。

地震と同じように，火山がいつ爆発するかを予知することは困難ですが，日本の火山観測体制はハワイと並んで世界でも優秀で，事前の活動の観測から，比較的早く警報を出すことができるようになってきています。

Q: 日本でいちばん長い川はどれですか？

日本でいちばん長い川は信濃川です。長野県東部から新潟県の中央部を流れて，最後は新潟市で日本海に注ぎこみます。

信濃川は水源から河口まで367kmで，ミシシッピー川の3,780km，ダニューブ川の2,860km，ライン川の1,320kmに比べると比較になりません。しかし，国の規模にしては比較的長い川です。

日本は山国なので急流の川が多く，その中には第2位の関東平野を流れる利根川，第3位の北海道の石狩川があります。

• When is Mt. Fuji likely to erupt?

The first recorded eruption of Mt. Fuji was in 781, and it is said to have erupted 13 times roughly once every 30 years till 1083.

An interval of 428 years elapsed before the 14th eruption, and only 3 eruptions were recorded between 1511 and 1707. Since then, no volcanic activities have been observed, which means Mt. Fuji has been in a dormant state. However, there still is the possibility of an eruption, no matter how slim.

As is the case with earthquakes, it is difficult to predict volcanic eruptions, but Japan's excellent observation system, equal to that of Hawaii, boasts of its quick response to volcanic activities making it possible to quickly issue warnings.

• What is the longest river in Japan?

Japan's longest river is the Shinano River, which starts in the eastern part of Nagano Prefecture, runs through central Niigata, and flows into the Sea of Japan at Niigata City.

The Shinano, 367 km from source to mouth, is not long at all compared with famous rivers in the world such as the Mississippi (3,780 km), the Danube (2,860 km), and the Rhine (1,320 km), but it is relatively long for the size of the country.

Japan is abundant with such short and fast-flowing rivers originating in the mountains, including the Tone River, the second longest, flowing through the Kantō Plain, and Hokkaidō's Ishikari River, the third longest river.

日本の気候

Q: 日本はどんな気候の国ですか？

最大の特徴は，春，夏，秋，冬の移り変わりが非常にはっきりしていることです。

一般に，3月，4月，5月が春，6月，7月，8月が夏，9月，10月，11月が秋，12月，1月，2月が冬とされています。

冬と夏との気温差は30度を超します。夏は高温である上に湿度が高いので，からっとした大陸性の気候に慣れた人は不快さを感じるでしょう。春と秋の気温は日本のほとんどどこでも快適な温度ですが，天気が安定しません。

夏の初めには北海道を除いて梅雨があり，6月から7月の半ばまで，雨の多い日が続きます。

秋も比較的に雨が多く，また，夏の終わりから秋の初めにかけては，北太平洋の西部で発生する台風にも見舞われ，大きな被害が出ることがあります。

また，山地が日本列島を日本海側と太平洋側に分けていて，冬は日本海側に多くの雪が降ることも日本の特徴です。

Q: 日本で雪が多いのはどこですか？

Snow country

亜熱帯の沖縄県は別として，日本は雪が降る地域が多い国です。これは，大陸から吹きつける冬の季節風が，日本全国を背骨のように走る山岳地帯にさえぎられて，北海道から本州の中部にかけての日本海側に雪を降らせるのです。

新潟県と福島県の県境や北陸地方の山間部

Climate of Japan

• What is the climate of Japan like?

The climate of most of Japan is characterized by four distinct seasons.

The spring months generally are from March to May, summer months are from June to August, autumn from September to November, and winter from December to February.

The difference between winter temperatures and summer temperatures is more than 30 degrees Celcius. Summer months, with high temperatures and high humidity, may be uncomfortable for those who are used to dry continental climate. In spring and autumn almost all parts of Japan enjoy a comfortable temperature, but the weather is very changeable.

All areas except Hokkaidō have a rainy season in the beginning of summer, which usually lasts from early June to mid-July.

Autumn is also a time of substantial precipitation. From the end of summer to the beginning of autumn, typhoons generated in the western part of the North Pacific Ocean hit the country, sometimes causing extensive damage.

Mountain ranges running almost the full length of Japan divide the archipelago into the Japan Sea side and the Pacific side. The Japan Sea side, has heavy snowfall in winter.

• Which part of Japan has the most snow?

Except for semitropical Okinawa, most parts of Japan have snow in winter. Northwesterly seasonal winds off the Asian continent, blocked by rugged mountains, bring heavy snows mainly on the Japan Sea side from Hokkaidō to the central part of Honshū.

On the borders between Niigata Prefecture and Fukushima

では，3mを超える積雪をみることは普通です。地球上でも最も積雪の多い地方の1つ，新潟県の山岳部では，昔8mを超えたという記録があるそうです。

Q: 日本でいちばんいい季節はいつですか？

10世紀に清少納言という女性作家が『枕草子』という随筆で，それぞれの季節に趣があると書いています。それには「春は曙（夜明け）がよく，夏は夜が，秋は夕暮れが，そして冬は早朝が，それぞれいい」と書いています。

このように季節それぞれに魅力がありますが，一般的には春と秋，特に5月初めの新緑のころと，紅葉の9月末か11月の半ばがいちばんいい季節だと感じる日本人が多いと思います。気候が安定していて，旅行などには最高のシーズンだからです。

日本の自然災害

Q: 日本に地震が多いのはなぜですか？

日本列島は北米プレートとユーラシアプレートの上にのっていますが，このプレートの下に，太平洋プレートとフィリピン海プレートがもぐりこんできています。そのために非常に地震が多いのです。

そして，日本の地層には，活断層と言われるものが随所に走っています。

活断層は，過去数十万年の間に何度も動いた形跡があり，今後もその可能性があると判断できる断層のことです。その活動は，約1,000年に1度ぐらいの周期だとも言われています。1995

Prefecture, and in the mountains of the Hokuriku region, snowfall of over 3 meters is not unusual. The heaviest snowfall on record is 8 meters in the mountains in Niigata Prefecture, one of the snowiest regions on earth.

• When is the best season in Japan?

Each season has its own charm, as Sei Shōnagon, a female author in the 10th century, wrote in her anthology of essays titled *Makura no Sōshi*. She says in her essays that dawn is best in spring, night is best in summer, twilight is best in autumn, and early morning is best in winter.

But the majority of the Japanese would say that the best seasons are spring and autumn, especially early May when trees are freshly green, and between late September and mid-November when the leaves change colors. The weather then is pleasant to fully enjoy traveling.

Natural Disasters in Japan

• Why does Japan have a lot of earthquakes?

The Japanese Archipelago is situated on the North American Plate and the Eurasian Plate. Squeezed in under these plates are the Pacific Plate and The Phillipines Sea Plate which makes the landforms unstable, causing a lot of earthquakes in and around the area.

There are many active faults in the strata that form the land of Japan.

An active fault is a fault that has shown traces of activity during the past several hundred thousand years, and is likely to start moving in the future. The cycle of its activity is said to be once every thousand years. The Great Hanshin-Awaji Earth-

年1月の阪神・淡路大震災は，この活断層による地震でした。

Q: 近年，どこで大地震が起こりましたか？

Great Hanshin-Awaji Earthquake

1995年1月17日午前5時46分に，大地震が兵庫県南部を襲いました。阪神・淡路大震災と名付けられた地震です。これまでの日本の大地震は，海溝近くのプレート境界面で起きることが多かったのですが，この地震は，神戸市の真下の活断層がずれて発生したものです。

阪神・淡路大震災は6,000人をこえる死者・行方不明者，4万人をこえる負傷者。家屋の損壊は20万戸にものぼる，史上最悪の大震災となりました。震源はマグニチュード7.2を記録しました。

古くは1923年に9万人の死者と10万人の負傷者を出した，震度7.9の関東大震災が有名ですが，90年代だけで，北海道と東北地方でいくつかの大地震が起こっています。

Q: これから大地震が起こりそうなところはどこですか？

明確な予知は，現在の科学技術をもってしても不可能ですが，過去のデータから危険と推定される所はいくつかあります。

静岡県の駿河湾を震源域と想定している「東海地震」は，極端にいえば，明日起こっても不思議ではないという説もあります。そのために，この地域は常時，観測されています。

東北地方の三陸沖も大地震の発生が心配されています。日本の下に太平洋プレートがもぐ

quake in January 1995, was caused by such active faults.

• Where did the latest large earthquake occur?

At 5:46 a.m. on January 17th, 1995, a major earthquake hit the southern part of Hyōgo Prefecture, which later was named "the Great Hanshin-Awaji Earthquake." Major earthquakes in Japan have often occurred on surfaces bordering plates near trenches, but this particular earthquake was generated by the movement of an active fault that runs under the city of Kōbe.

The Great Hanshin-Awaji Earthquake became one of the most devastating earthquakes in history, with a death toll exceeding 6,000. More than 40,000 people were injured, and 200,000 houses collapsed. It recorded a magnitude of 7.2 on the Japanese scale.

In 1923 there was a major temblor of a similar magnitude called the "Tōkyō Earthquake of 1923," measuring a magnitude of 7.9, killing 90,000 and injuring 100,000. In the 1990's alone, several major earthquakes have occurred in Hokkaidō and the Tōhoku regions.

• Are there any areas likely to have major earthquakes in the near future?

There are several areas considered dangerous based on data accumulated over a long period of time, although precise prediction of earthquakes is said to be impossible with today's scientific technology.

Some specialists say that a major earthquake could occur at any moment in Suruga Bay in Shizuoka Prefecture located in the Tōkai region. This area is being constantly monitored.

Off the coast of Sanriku in the Tōhoku region is another area to which much attention is being paid, because the Pacific

りこんできているところだからです。海に面しているこの地域の地震では津波の心配もあるので，要注意です。

活断層は全国各地にありますが，特に，中部地方，近畿地方に多いようです。東京では北西部から東の方に向けて，比較的に大きい活断層があります。いずれも地震の可能性があると言えるでしょう。

Q: 英語になっているtsunamiとは何ですか？

津波は，おもに地震によって一気に変化した海底の地形の影響で押し寄せる高い波のことをいいます。歴史的に見れば，日本のほとんどの海岸が，これまで津波に襲われた過去を持っています。ことに，東北地方の三陸海岸に被害が目立ちます。

この原因は，三陸海岸はリアス式海岸で，小さな湾は岸壁の奥に食い込んだようにして存在していますので，湾に達するときには津波の高さが大きくなっているからです。

1993年の北海道南西沖地震では，奥尻島に最大20mもの高さの津波が襲来し，死者・不明者が230人という被害をだす一因となりました。

Q: 台風は1年にどれくらい来るのですか？

大ざっぱに言って，台風は平均して年4回，日本を襲っています。台風は北太平洋の西部で発生しますが，その数は，過去の平均では27個ぐらいです。そのすべてが日本に向かってく

Plate is in the process of squeezing itself under the Japanese Islands, making this area prone to temblors. There is also the possibility of *tsunami*, or tidal wave, should an earthquake hit this region which faces the sea.

Active fault lines run throughout the nation, but a number of them exist in the Chūbu and Kinki regions. Tōkyō is no exception, with a relatively large active fault running from its northwestern part toward the east. Wherever there is an active fault, earthquakes are possible.

• What is *tsunami*, a word used in English?

Tsunami is a high tidal wave generated by a shift in the ocean floor, which is in most cases caused by an earthquake. Much of the Japanese seacoast has experienced *tsunami*. Among them, the Sanriku coast in the Tōhoku region has particularly suffered extensive damage.

The reason, scientists assume, is the formation of a ria coastline, consisting of a multitude of narrow and complicated bays, which may make the *tsunami* wave even higher.

Immediately after the earthquake off the southwestern coast of Hokkaidō in 1993, a major *tsunami* with a maximum height of 20 meters, hit the coast of Okushiri Island. The number of the dead and the missing caused by the *tsunami* totaled 230.

• How often does Japan have typhoons?

Roughly speaking, 4 typhoons on the average hit the nation annually. The average number of typhoons born in the western part of the North Pacific Ocean is 27 per year. Not all of them head for Japan because of the influences of seasonal upper

Typhoon

るわけではありません。台風を移動させる上層の風の流れが，発生した季節によって異なるからです。

冬や春に発生する台風は，貿易風に乗って西に進み，日本には来ません。ところが，夏や秋に発生した台風は，太平洋高気圧の西縁をめぐって北に向かい，日本を襲うことが多くなるのです。

Q: 台風とハリケーンはどこが違うのでしょう?

ハリケーンは，北大西洋とインド洋に発生する熱帯低気圧で，最大風速が秒速32.7m以上の暴風雨です。

台風は，北太平洋西部で発生する熱帯低気圧で，最大風速が秒速17.2m以上の暴風雨のことをいいます。台風の語源は「大きな風」を意味する中国語の“taifung”だと言われています。

発生場所と最大風速のとらえ方の違いこそあれ，その性質は台風もハリケーンも基本的には同じものです。

layer winds that move typhoons.

Typhoons in spring and winter go west on the trade winds and never land in Japan, but those in summer and autumn go around the west end of the high pressure system in the Pacific Ocean, and in many cases end up going in the direction of Japan.

• What is the difference between typhoons and hurricanes?

A hurricane is a tropical cyclone that develops in the North Atlantic Ocean and the Indian Ocean, and is defined as a rainstorm with a maximum wind speed of over 32.7 meters per second.

A typhoon is a tropical cyclone that develops in the western part of the North Pacific Ocean, and refers to a rainstorm with a maximum wind speed of over 17.2 meters per second. The origin of the word "typhoon" is said to be the Chinese word "taifung," which means big wind.

The nature of typhoons and hurricanes is basically the same, although they differ in the place they are born, and the way their wind speed is defined.

2

日本のルーツと歴史

日本の誕生

Q: 日本という国はいつごろ誕生したのですか?

七八十年倭國亂相攻
王名曰卑彌呼事鬼道
有男弟佐治國自爲王

The Account of the Wa People

日本では2月11日が「建国記念の日」とされています。これは『古事記』や『日本書紀』という古文書に書かれた神話伝承に基づくものですが，学問上，史実かどうかということには疑問が残ります。

日本には5世紀以前の文献はなく，中国の資料によるほうがわかりやすいようです。中国の『後漢書』には，57年に「日本の奴国（なこく）の王が使節をよこした」と，そして『魏史倭人伝』には「邪馬台国（やまたいこく）に卑弥呼（ひみこ）という女王がいて，30ほどの国をまとめていた」という記述があります。

『日本書紀』では，この卑弥呼が神功（じんぐう）皇后であるとしていますが，現在の古代歴史学では否定されており，邪馬台国が滅びた後，7世紀ご

2

ORIGIN AND HISTORY OF JAPAN

Birth of Japan

• When did Japan emerge as a nation?

In Japan, February 11th is regarded as National Foundation Day. This date is based on legends chronicled in the ancient texts *Kojiki* and *Nihon shoki*, but from an academic perspective, there is doubt over its historical accuracy.

Since Japan has no written records prior to the fifth century, we can probably learn more from Chinese texts. According to the Chinese text *Gokanjo* (History of the Later Han Dynasty), in the year 57 A.D. "the king of the Japanese kingdom of Na dispatched a mission (to China)," while "The Account of the Wa People" in the *Wei zhi* (The Wei Chronicle) contains a reference to "a queen named Himiko in the land of Yamatai, who ruled over about thirty countries."

Although the *Nihon shoki* regards Himiko as Empress Jingū, historians dispute this claim. It could be that following its decline, Yamatai by the seventh century was unified into

ろまでに，1つの国としてのまとまりができ，これが大和（やまと）政権の始まりと考えられます。

Q：日本をニホン，あるいはニッポンと呼ぶようになったのはいつごろからですか？

『日本書紀』や『古事記』によると，古い時代の日本のことを「豊葦原瑞穂国（とよあしはらみずほのくに）」とか，「葦原中国（あしはらなかつくに）」と呼んでいます。しかし，中国や韓国では古代日本を「倭（わ）」と称していました。日本ではこれを「ヤマト」と言っていました。

ところが，しばらく中国との交渉が途絶えていた後，7世紀の初め，中国の『旧唐書（くとうじょ）』という書物に，次の文句が登場します。「日本国は倭国の別種なり。その国，日の辺に在るを以ての故に，日本を以て名と為す」，「倭国自らその名の雅（みやび）ならざるを悪（にく）み，改めて日本と為す」

「日本」の登場です。

『日本書紀』は8世紀の編集ですので，それまでの資料に使われていた「倭国」が，「日本」に書き換えられていったに違いありません。

Q：日本は「ニホン」か「ニッポン」，どちらが正しい言い方ですか？

1934年，文部省の臨時国語審議会が「ニッポン」を正式の呼び方としています。それまでもバラバラだったわけです。しかし，この決定は法律として制定されたわけではなく，今でもどちらの言い方も通用しています。

切手には Nippon と印刷されていますし，日本が海外に派遣するスポーツ団のユニホームなども Nippon が多いので，公式には「ニッポン」が認められているといっていいでしょう。

one polity, which then served as the basis for Yamato rule.

• How did Japan come to be called "Nihon" or "Nippon"?

In the *Nihon shoki* and the *Kojiki*, ancient Japan is referred to as "Toyoashiharamizuho no kuni" and "Ashiharanakatsu kuni." However, in China and Korea, ancient Japan was called "Wa" (*Wo* in Chinese), while Japan referred to itself as "Yamato."

However, the following passage appeared in the Chinese *Jiu Tang shu* in the beginning of the 7th century, following a temporary cessation in Japan's relations with China: 'Nihon-koku' (*Ribenguo* in Chinese) is distinct from 'Wa-koku' (*Woguo* in Chinese). This country is named 'Nihon' because it exists near the sun. It has been renamed 'Nihon' since the people of 'Wa-koku' disliked the inelegance of their name.

Thus was the dawn of "Nihon."

Since the *Nihon shoki* was compiled in the 8th century, it most likely had revised previously existing materials so that all references to "Wa-koku" were replaced with "Nihon."

• Is it correct to refer to Japan as "Nihon" or "Nippon"?

In 1934, the Ministry of Education's Provisional Deliberation Council on the Japanese Language designated "Nippon" as the official name. Until this time, usage was random. However, the use of "Nippon" was not decreed by law, and even today, both names are commonly used.

Since postage stamps are marked "Nippon" and Japanese athletes sent overseas often wear uniforms emblazoned "Nippon," it can be said that "Nippon" is regarded as the official name for Japan.

Q: 日本人はどこから来たのですか？

日本人は人種的に純粋であると信じている人がいますが，現在の研究では，日本人はその身体的な特徴から，いくつかの種族の混合だと言われています。

とすると，どんな人種が混合したのかということになりますが，東南アジアから海を渡ってきた種族（縄文タイプ），朝鮮半島を経由してきたツングース系の種族（弥生タイプ），そしてアイヌ系の種族などが，長い間に混じり合って日本人を作っていったものと考えられます。

Q: アイヌ民族はいつごろから日本にいたのですか？

Traditional wear of the Ainu

今から約1000年ほど前，樺太（からふと），千島列島，北海道および本州の北部に広がる擦文（さつもん）文化圏を作っていた民族がアイヌだと言われています。アイヌのほうが先住民族なのです。

アイヌは狩猟，漁猟，植物の採集など，自然に依存した生活をしていましたが，15世紀ごろから，アイヌ人たちが「和人」と呼んだ日本人が北海道に侵入を始め，住んでいた広大な自然環境を奪われていきます。

激しい衝突が繰り返された結果，18世紀末には，北海道のアイヌは日本の支配下に入ってしまうことになりました。

その後，明治政府になってからは，内地人との同化政策がとられ，アイヌ民族としての存在は脅かされていきました。しかし、アイヌ文化，アイヌ語は，今日も子孫たちによって守られています。

• Where did the Japanese people come from?

Although there are people who believe in the racial purity of the Japanese, current studies hold that the physical features of the Japanese people reveal their derivation from a mixture of several ethnic groups.

Then, what racial groups comprised this admixture? We can say that the Japanese stock was created over a long period of time, by the gradual mixture of the "Jōmon strain," an ethnic group from Southeast Asia that had crossed the sea to Japan, the "Yayoi strain," a Tungusic people arriving through the Korean peninsula, and the Ainu ethnic group.

• How long have the Ainu people inhabited Japan?

It is commonly held that the Ainu are the ethnic group that about a thousand years ago established the "*Satsumon* culture," which encompassed a region spanning Sakhalin, the Kuril Islands, Hokkaidō, and northern Honshū. The Ainu are the aboriginal people of Japan.

The Ainu were long dependent upon nature, making their livelihood out of hunting, fishing, and gathering, However, beginning in the 15th century with invasions by the Japanese, whom the Ainu called *Wajin*, the Ainu's vast natural lands were gradually confiscated from them.

By around the 18th century, a series of viscious clashes had led to the complete subjugation of the Ainu people by the Japanese.

Following the establishment of the Meiji government, policies encouraging assimilation with mainstream Japanese were implemented, which proceeded to threaten the existence of the Ainu as an ethnic group. However, the Ainu culture and language is today guarded by Ainu descendants.

日本の国歌・国旗

Q: 君が代はいつ制定されたのですか?

1893年(明治26年),文部省から,初等教育において祝日の儀式に際して歌うべき歌として公布されています。

実は,日本国歌の必要を説いたのはイギリス人軍楽隊長のフェントンという人で,歌詞には『古今和歌集』『和漢朗詠集』の中にある読み人知らずのこの歌が選ばれました。

そして何度かメロディーが検討された末,1880年に雅楽家の林広守(はやしひろもり)の旋律が採用され,ドイツ人音楽教師エッケルトが編曲し,今の君が代が完成しています。

しかしその後の,日清戦争,日露戦争,満州事変,そして太平洋戦争などという不幸な歴史の中で,軍国主義化した国の国歌となった君が代には,戦後,風当たりが強くなりました。軍国主義,天皇制の象徴として君が代を拒否する人たちが続出したのです。

不思議なことですが,事実上,日本の国歌として歌われていながら,法律で規定されているわけではありません。

Q: 君が代の歌詞はどんな意味ですか?

歌詞はこうなっています。

君が代は
千代に八千代に

Japan's National Anthem and National Flag

• When was *Kimigayo* established as the national anthem?

In 1893 (26th year of Meiji), the Ministry of Education decreed that *Kimigayo* would be incorporated into primary education as the anthem to be sung at ceremonies honoring national holidays.

Actually, the person who stressed the need for establishing a Japanese national anthem was a British military band leader named Fenton; the words for the song came from a poem in the *Kokinwakashū* and the *Wakanrōeishū*.

After much deliberation over the selection of a melody, a melody by the *gagaku* (ancient court music) composer Hayashi Hiromori was adopted in 1880, and then arranged by the German music educator Franz Eckert to constitute today's *Kimigayo*.

However, during the adverse course of history that followed, which saw the Sino-Japanese War, the Russo-Japanese War, the Manchurian Incident and the Pacific War, the national anthem took on militarist overtones, which exposed it to a wave of criticism in the postwar period. An increasing number of people came to dismiss *Kimigayo* as a symbol of militarism and the emperor system.

Strangely enough, while *Kimigayo* is sung as the de facto national anthem, it was never legally decreed as such.

• What do the words to *Kimigayo* mean?

These are the lyrics to *Kimigayo*:

The thousands of years of happy reign be thine;
Rule on, my Lord, till what are pebbles now

さざれ石の
巌(いわお)となりて
苔のむすまで

「君」という言葉は,「主人,家の長,友人,愛人」の意味で,現代語でも,親しい相手あるいは目下の人に対して,「君」と呼び掛けたりします。しかし,軍国主義の時代にはこの「君」は「天皇」に直接結びついていました。

歌詞全体の意味は,簡単に言えば,「いつまでも元気で!」「末長く!」といった意味ですから,これから問題になるとすれば,歌詞が文語だし,メロディーも8ビートに慣れた若者たちには,いかにも悠長に聞こえてしまうということでしょう。新しい国歌を……という声も出ています。

Q: 日本の国旗,日の丸はいつ制定されたのですか?

実は,君が代と同様に,日の丸(日章旗)を日本の国旗とする……という法的な規定はなにひとつないのです。

白地に赤い円を描いた現在のデザインは,

日本の国歌と国旗

By age united to mighty rocks shall grow
Whose venerable sides the moth doth line.

Kimi can mean "lord, household head, friend, lover." In modern Japanese *kimi* is used to address a new companion or a subordinate. But during the militarist period, *kimi* also was directly associated with the Emperor.

The overall meaning of the words, simply stated, is somewhat similar to "To your good health! And long life!" The problem then would probably lie in the fact that the lyrics are antiquated, and the melody too slow for young people accustomed to eight-beat melodies. There are those pushing for the adoption of a new national anthem.

• When was the national flag adopted?

In actual fact, similar to the case of the national anthem, there are no laws designating the Rising Sun as the national flag.

The current design—a red disc in the center of a white

National Anthem and Flag

● 日の丸 Hinomaru

The vertical to horizontal ratio is set at 2 : 3, the disc is to be placed at the exact center, and the diameter of the disc is to equal three-fifths of the vertical measurement of the flag.

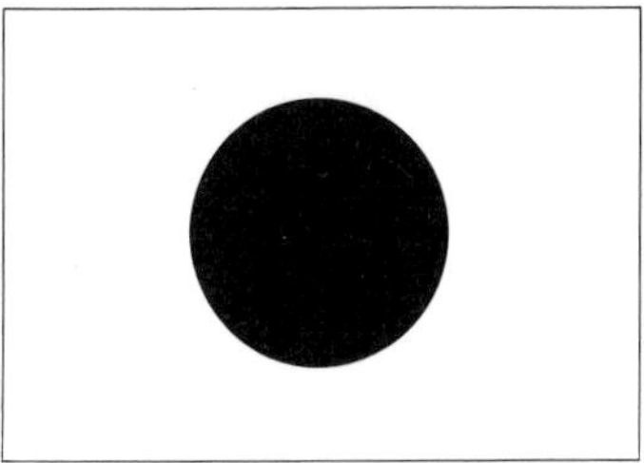

1854年，徳川幕府が日本の船の船印として取り入れたものです。これは日本の船を外国の船と区別するためのもので，必ずしも日本の国旗というわけではなかったのです。

明治時代になり，1870年には太政官(だじょうかん)布告でこの船印の規格を制定していますが，その後，いつのまにか国旗として定着してしまいました。

日の丸も，軍国主義の名の下に誤った道をたどった日本を象徴することになりましたので，太平洋戦争後，君が代と同様，日の丸を拒否する人たちもいます。

Q: 日本の国の花は何ですか？

Chrysanthemum

法律で定められた国花はありません。しかし皇室の紋章であるキクか，または，国民に愛好されているサクラが日本の国の花と言われています。

国花には中国のウメのように法律で制定されたものもありますが，フランスのユリやアイリス，イギリスのバラやスイセンといったように自然にきまったものが多いようです。

Q: 日本の国鳥は何ですか？

日の丸，君が代と同じく，これも法的に規定されたことはありません。

一応，キジが日本の国鳥ということになっていますが，これは1947年，日本鳥学会の第81回例会で選ばれたものです。

キジが選ばれたのは，緑色のキジは日本固有の種であり，また，日本の民話の中にもたく

field—was originally adopted by the Tokugawa government in 1854 to be used on flags for Japan's ships. This was done in order to distinguish Japanese ships from foreign ships, and was not necessarily intended to stand as Japan's national flag.

During the Meiji period, in the year 1870, a proclamation issued by the *Dajōkan* (Grand Council of State) government adopted this as the standard flag for ships, and this over time became accepted as the national flag.

As the Rising Sun has come to symbolize a Japan that once traversed an erroneous militarist path, there are now in the postwar period a number of people who, as with *Kimigayo*, reject the Rising Sun.

• What is the national flower of Japan?

There is no legally designated national flower. However, the chrysanthemum, the crest of the imperial family, and the cherry blossom so loved by the Japanese, are commonly regarded as the national flowers of Japan.

While there are national flowers like China's plum blossom that have been designated by law, there are also many such as France's lily and iris, or Britain's rose and daffodil, that have come to be accepted informally.

• What is the national bird of Japan?

Like the Rising Sun, and *Kimigayo*, the Japanese pheasant (*kiji*) has never been legally designated as the national bird of Japan.

While the pheasant is now regarded as the national bird of Japan, it originally was designated as such in 1947 at the 81st Meeting of the National Bird Society of Japan.

The Japanese pheasant, or *kiji*, was most likely selected because this green pheasant is unique to Japan, and further-

さん登場し，日本の風土に根づいている鳥であるからでしょう。

日本語

Q: 日本語はどこから来たのですか？

日本語がいちばん似ている言語は朝鮮語です。確かに主語・目的語・述語の並び方などの共通点があります。しかし，まだ，同系の言語であるという証明はされていません。

日本語はウラル・アルタイ語族の1つではないか，南方系のマライ・ポリネシア語族ではないか，チベット・インドの諸語と関係があるのではないか，タミル語と同系ではないかとか，実にいろいろな説があります。

起源はわかりませんが，言語としては，中国との文化的な交流の中から，中国語の語彙を多数，日本語の中に受け入れ，さらに漢字の中国字音から平仮名，片仮名を作りだすなどして，漢字と仮名で構成される日本語が作られていきました。

Q: 日本語の特徴はどこにありますか？

まず発音の特徴ですが，基本的に1つの音(おん)は，「ん(n)」を除いて，母音だけ，あるいは子音＋母音で表されます。

時計(とけい)→ to-ke-i
私(わたくし)→ wa-ta-ku-shi
元気(げんき)→ gen-ki

アクセントは英語のような強弱アクセントではなく，高低アクセントで，横浜［ヨコハマ］の［ヨ］

more because it appears often in Japanese folktales and so has become an integral part of the Japanese cultural landscape.

Japanese Language

• What are the origins of the Japanese language?

The closest language to Japanese is Korean. There are definite commonalities in the arrangement of the subject, direct object, and predicate. However, there is no determining evidence that they belong to the same linguistic family.

There are many theories about the origins of the Japanese language: Japanese has been posited to be one of the Ural-Altaic languages; one of the southern, Malayo-Polynesian languages; a relative to the Indo-Tibetan languages; or one of the Tamil languages.

While its origins remain uncertain, the Japanese language did incorporate many Chinese words. The *hiragana* and *katakana* syllabaries were created based on the Chinese readings for the characters, resulting in a language that incorporated both Chinese characters and *kana* syllabaries.

• What are the distinguishing features of Japanese?

First of all, regarding its pronunciation, Japanese consists primarily of syllables which, with the exception of ん ("n") are made up of either single vowels, or consonant + vowel pairs.

tokei (a clock, a watch) → to-ke-i
watakushi (I, my, me) → wa-ta-ku-shi
genki (vigor, cheerful) → gen-ki

Japanese has no strong stress accent like that of English but rather has a high-low pitch accent, such that when pronounc-

は低く[コハマ]は少し高く発音します。

しかし，アクセントは日本全国同じというわけではなく，西日本と東日本で，また地域で異なる語がたくさんあります。

日本語の語彙は，和語（大和言葉）と言われる日本固有の語と，漢語から取り入れた語，そして現代では，外国語から取り入れたカタカナ語から成り立っています。

文章は，基本的に

1)主語＋補語＋述語動詞
　彼は＋大学生＋です。
2)主語＋目的語＋述語動詞
　私は＋アイスクリームを＋食べた。

という形をしていますが，述語が文末に来ること，修飾語は必ず被修飾語の前に来ることを守れば，語順は比較的自由です。

英語などに比べて特徴があるのは，韓国語と同様に，敬語が高度に発達していることです。また，会話では男性語と女性語の区別が明瞭であることも特徴です。

Q: 平仮名，片仮名はどうしてできたのですか？

仮名は，漢字が持っている意味を捨てて，その読み方（発音）を簡単な形にして表したものということができます。実例を上げてみましょう。

以(i) → 以 → い → い
加(ka) → 加 → か → か
礼(rei) → 礼 → 礼 → れ

ing the word Yokohama: the "Yo" sound is relatively low, while "kohama" is pronounced at a slightly higher pitch.

However, this accent system is not applied uniformly throughout Japan, as seen in the regional variations between eastern and western Japan. There are also many words that vary by region as well.

The Japanese vocabulary consists of native words, *wago* or *yamato kotoba*; words adopted from Chinese; and in the modern period, *katakana*-words that have been used for foreign loan words.

The basic sentence structure is as follows:

(1) Subject + Complement + Predicate
  *He + university student + is.
(2) Subject + Object + Predicate
  *I + ice cream + ate.

As long as the predicate comes at the end of the sentence, and the modifier always precedes the subordinate modifier, the arrangement of words is relatively free.

Like Korean, but in contrast to English, Japanese has very developed polite forms. Another feature is that spoken Japanese has distinctive male and female forms of speech.

• How did the *hiragana* and *katakana* syllabaries originate?

We might say that *kana* do not convey the meaning of *kanji*, but rather stand for their simplified sounds. Let's take a look at the following examples.

以(i) → 以 → 以 → い
加(ka) → 加 → か → か
礼(rei) → 礼 → 礼 → れ

漢字が平仮名に変えられていく姿がわかると思います。

8世紀の中ごろ編集された万葉集は，和歌が4,500首ほど収録されていますが，すべて，漢字に当てた音で表されています。

その後，次第に上記の例のように漢字が簡略されていき，9世紀の終わりには，現在のような平仮名の字体が出来上がりました。

片仮名は平仮名がさらに単純化されたもので，平仮名と並行して作られ，9世紀の初頭にはすでに使われている文献があります。

そして，平仮名は書簡文や物語文などに，また片仮名は漢文の難しい文字の読みや注釈に使われていきます。

Q：漢字はいくつ覚えればいいのですか？

漢字の字の種類は，約5万もあると言われています。その中から多くの漢字が日本語に取り入れられ，また，峠（とうげ），裃（かみしも）など，日本で作られた漢字も出てきました。

しかし，日常生活でたくさんの漢字が必要なわけではありませんので，現在では1,945字が一般的に使用する「常用漢字」の目安として選定されています。

Q：漢字，平仮名，片仮名はどのように使いますか？

日本語には3つの文字の形があります。漢字，平仮名，片仮名です。漢字は中国から取り入れられた象形文字です。平仮名と片仮名は漢字の読みを表すもので，漢字を簡略化して作られています。

多くの名詞は漢字で書かれており，動詞と形

You can see in this diagram the process by which *kanji* are transformed into *hiragana*.

The *Manyōshū*, which was compiled in the mid-8th century, contains about 4,500 *waka* poems; yet most are written with *kanji* which had been randomly assigned sounds.

Over time, *kanji* were simplified, and by the end of the 9th century, they had evolved into the current *hiragana* syllabary.

Katakana, which are even more simple than *hiragana*, developed alongside the *hiragana* syllabary, and was already used in written works by the beginning of the 9th century.

Hiragana came to be used in correspondences and narratives, while *katakana* was used for annotations and as phonetic symbols for difficult *kanji*.

• How many *kanji* must one learn?

There are said to be some 50,000 *kanji*, most of which have been adopted into Japanese. There are also *kanji*, such as 峠 *tōge* (mountain pass) and 裃 *kamishimo* (old ceremonial dress), which were created in Japan.

However, many *kanji* are not necessarily used in daily life, and today, 1,945 characters have been designated as *jōyō kanji*, or *kanji* in common use.

• How are the Japanese characters, or *kanji*, *hiragana*, and *katakana* used?

There are three traditional characters in the Japanese language: *kanji*, *hiragana*, and *katakana*. *Kanji* are ideograms brought from China. *Hiragana* and *katakana*, which phonetically represent readings of *kanji*, were later made by simplifying *kanji*.

Many nouns are written in *kanji*, verbs and adjectives are

容詞の多くは漢字と平仮名混じりで書かれます。助詞や助動詞は平仮名，外来語は片仮名で書かれます。

例えば,「私は動物園でパンダを見た」という文では，名詞の「私」「動物園」，動詞の「見た」の「見」は，通例，漢字で書きます。上のように意味がはっきりしている場合には，全部平仮名で書くこともできます。

しかし，日本語にはたくさんの同音異義語がありますので，意味の理解のためには，表意文字である漢字を入れるほうがいいとされています。

Q: 日本語の文は縦書き，横書き，どっちが多いんですか？

日本に残された歴史的な文献はすべてが縦に書かれています。昔は日本語は縦書きだけだったのです。

しかし，西洋の文献が流入してきて，アルファベット，アラビア数字，数学の公式などを取り入れるとなると，どうも縦書きでは具合が悪いのです。

幸い，漢字と仮名は個々に意味と働きを持っているものですから，縦に並べても，横に並べても意味は通じますから，数字や横文字を多用しなければならない自然科学関係の文は，次第に横書きになっていきます。今では学校の教科書も，国語・古文などを除いて，ほとんどが横書きになっています。

店頭に並ぶ一般の出版物の多くは縦組みですが，若い人たちは，横に読むこと，横に書くことには全く抵抗はなく，横書きがますます増えてくることは間違いありません。

written mostly in *kanji-hiragana* combination, particles and auxiliary verbs in *hiragana*, and loan words in *katakana*.

For example, in the sentence "watashi wa dōbutsuen de panda o mita" (I saw a panda at the zoo), "watashi" (I = noun), "dōbutsuen" (zoo = noun), "mi" of "mita" (part of the verb 'saw') are usually written in *kanji*. Sentences, when their meaning is clear enough as in the above case, may also be written all in *hiragana*.

However, since there are thousands of homonyms in Japanese, it was decided that *kanji* be included for clarification purposes because *kanji* is ideographic.

• Is Japanese text more commonly written vertically or horizontally?

All extant historical documents in Japan are written vertically. Long ago, Japanese was only written vertically.

However, with the introduction of Western written materials and the need to accommodate the alphabet, arabic numerals, and mathematical formulas, the vertical style seemed ill-suited.

Fortunately, since each individual *kanji* and *kana* has its own meaning and function, they could be arranged vertically or horizontally without losing their meaning. Science-related text, which required the use of numbers and foreign words, gradually came to be written in the horizontal style. Today, most school textbooks—with the exception of subjects such as Japanese or classical literature—are set in horizontal text.

Most general books sold in stores are set in vertical text. However, as young people today find no difficulty reading or writing Japanese in horizontal lines, this style undoubtedly will become increasingly common in the future.

日本の天皇

Q: だれが日本の最初の天皇になったのですか?

Nintoku Mausoleum

『古事記』や『日本書紀』という日本の古代歴史を記録した本によりますと,日本の初代の天皇は神武(じんむ)天皇となっています。紀元前660年のこととされています。

しかし,事実として証明されたことではなく,『古事記』『日本書紀』共に8世紀になってから編纂されたものですから,神話として作られたものという説が有力です。

実在した可能性があるのは,第10代の崇神(すじん)天皇からと言われますが,記録が残っているのは,592年から628年まで在位した第33代推古天皇からです。この時代,皇太子として聖徳太子が登場しています。

Q: 天皇のルーツはどこにありますか?

日本民族がどこから来たのかもわかりませんし,日本誕生自体がナゾなのですから,天皇のルーツもわかっていません。邪馬台国の卑弥呼がその祖先であるという説,邪馬台国と対抗していたと言われる狗奴国(くなこく)の末裔(まつえい)であるという説,大和地方の豪族の1つの祖先であるという説……いろいろです。

しかし,いずれにしてもいくつかの国が勢力を競い合っていた中で,大和(やまと)朝廷と言われるまでの存在になったどこかの勢力の子孫であるというわけです。

Q: 日本にはこれまで何人の天皇がいましたか?

もちろん歴史的事実はわかりませんが,『日本

The Emperor of Japan

• Who was the first emperor of Japan?

According to the ancient historical chronicles, the *Kojiki* and the *Nihon shoki*, Japan's first emperor was supposedly Emperor Jimmu, who lived around 660 B.C.

However, this has not been proven to be true; it is widely held that the *Kojiki* and *Nihon shoki* are based on legend, as both were compiled only after the 8th century.

Although it is often said that the tenth emperor, Sujin, was possibly the first historical emperor, it is not until the 33rd emperor, Suiko, who reigned from 592–628, that actual records can be found. It was during this period that Prince Shōtoku emerged as the imperial prince.

• What are the origins of the imperial line?

Just as it is unclear where the Japanese people came from, or how Japan as a nation emerged, the origins of the imperial line are also unknown. There are many hypotheses: that Himiko of the Yamatai polity was the direct ancestor of the emperor; or that the emperor was descended from Yamatai's rival polity, *Kunakoku*; or that the emperor was descended from a powerful clan from the Yamato region.

Yet, despite the different theories, what seems to be true is that the imperial line descended from a regime that would eventually lay claim to the Yamato Court following a power struggle among a number of polities.

• How many Japanese emperors have there been altogether?

Of course it is impossible to know with historical accuracy,

書紀』『古事記』に書かれた神武(じんむ)天皇から数えると，平成の天皇は125代ということになります。

Q: 平成の天皇はどういう人ですか？

Emperor and Empress of Japan
©JAMP

1945年の太平洋戦争の敗戦により，天皇の地位は大きく変わります。新憲法によって，これまでの国の「元首」から，国の「象徴」と言われる存在となりました。この大きな変動のさなかに居たのは，現天皇の父の昭和天皇です。

太平洋戦争終結時には天皇は11歳でした。そして，アメリカ軍の駐留の下に，日本に民主主義が取り入れられた中で，これまでの帝王教育とは異なり，英語の教師としてアメリカからバイニング夫人を招くなど，新しい教育を受けられています。

皇族以外の人を皇太子妃に迎えたことも異例でしょう。しかも，軽井沢のテニスコートで見そめたというのですから，ほほえましいではありませんか。

1989年，昭和天皇の跡を継いで天皇となりますが，平和主義に徹したおだやかな人柄ということができます。

Q: 元号はどうやって決めるのですか？

昔は，天皇の崩御による新天皇即位の場合だけでなく，生前の退位や，天変地異などの災厄を避ける祈願のため，また，幕府の将軍の交代の時などに年号が改められました。

しかし，明治に年号が改まったときに，天皇

but if we begin with Emperor Jimmu chronicled in the *Nihon shoki* and *Kojiki*, the current Emperor would be the 125th reigning monarch.

• What sort of person is the current Emperor?

With the defeat of Japan in the Pacific War in 1945, the status of the emperor underwent a drastic change. According to the new constitution, the emperor was transformed from the head of state to a symbol of the state. The person who stood at the middle of this profound transformation was the Shōwa emperor, father of the current Emperor, Akihito.

The Emperor was 11 years old at the end of the Pacific War. And, while democracy was being introduced to Japan under the occupation by American forces, in contrast to past emperors, he was given a new education, which included his tutelage in English under an American instructor, Elizabeth Vining, sent from the U.S.

It was also a break from tradition when a person outside the royal family became the Crown Princess. And, it is even more heartwarming to know that the Crown Prince fell in love with his future princess on a tennis court in Karuizawa.

In 1989, the Crown Prince succeeded the Shōwa emperor to become the emperor. He can be described as a man of a gentle disposition who stands firmly for peace.

• How are era names determined?

Long ago, era names were changed not only upon the accession of a new emperor following the death of an emperor, but could also be changed during the reign of an emperor, for such reasons as to ward off natural disasters or upon the succession of a new *shōgun* to the *Bakufu* government.

However, when the new era name for the Meiji period was

の在位は即位から崩御までと定められました。太平洋戦争後の1947年5月3日から施行された日本国憲法で，天皇は「国の象徴」という存在になりましたが，在位についてはその定めに従っています。

ただし元号は，これまでは天皇の決定によるものでしたが，現在では，内閣が元号を定めることになっています。

新天皇の即位が決まると，内閣は有識者に新年号案の提出を求め，その案の中から決定をします。「平成」という年号は，初めてこの新しい方法で定められたものです。

Q: 今の天皇はどんな仕事をしているのですか?

1947年の日本国憲法の施行によって，天皇の存在は戦前と全く異なりました。明治維新以降に強化された天皇の統治権と神権はなくなり，「日本国の象徴」という存在になります。そして，天皇の仕事は，憲法に定められた「内閣の承認のもとに行う国事行為」に限られることになりました。

具体的には，総理大臣・最高裁判所長官の任命，国会の開会・解散の告示，法典の公布などです。

また，国民的行事への出席，海外からの各国元首との親善的な応接，外国への親善訪問など，政治的な影響を及ぼさない範囲で，積極的に国民と外国との融和に努力をしているのも，仕事ということができるでしょう。

established, it was determined that the emperor's reign would begin from the time of accession and continue until his death. In the Japanese Constitution that was promulgated on May 3, 1947 following the end of the Pacific War, the emperor was turned into a "symbol of the state," but the provisions regarding imperial reign were left unchanged.

Until this time, era names had been decreed by the emperor; however, it is the cabinet that today determines era names.

When the accession of a new emperor is determined, the cabinet seeks from various opinion leaders their proposals for a new era name, and selects one from among these proposals. The era name "Heisei" was the first selected under this new system.

• What sort of work does the current Emperor engage in?

Owing to a decree in the 1946 Japanese Constitution, the emperor's role was completely transformed. The sovereignty and divinity of the emperor, which was strengthened following the Meiji Restoration, was abolished, and the emperor became the "symbol of the Japanese state." And, as stipulated in the constitution, the emperor's role was confined to serving in "state functions approved by the cabinet."

Specifically, these functions include ceremonies marking the appointment of the Prime Minister and Chief Judge of the Supreme Court, the opening and closing of Diet sessions, and the promulgation of new laws.

It can also be added that his other function is to actively strive to harmonize relations between Japan and other countries through nonpolitical means by attending state ceremonies, welcoming foreign heads of state, and paying goodwill visits to foreign countries.

Q: 女性も天皇になれるのですか？

記録に残る歴代の天皇の中に，女性が10人ほどいます。いちばん古くは推古天皇(592–628)，いちばん新しくは後桜町(ごさくらまち)天皇（1762–70）です。

天皇は世襲制で，男系の男子が継ぐという形で継承順位が決まっていきますが，先代の天皇が没した後，即位の条件をみたした皇位継承者がなかった場合，先代天皇の皇后，皇女，あるいは皇太子妃が即位したことがあったようです。

1995年の10月現在，天皇には皇太子と秋篠宮(あきしののみや)という2人の子息が健在です。しかし，皇太子にはまだ子供がなく，秋篠宮の子供は2人とも女児ですから，現在は皇位継承の順位は，皇太子，秋篠宮，今上天皇の弟，常陸宮，昭和天皇の弟，三笠宮の順となります。しかし，そのどなたもが男児を遺さなかった場合、皇后あるいは皇女の継承もありうることになります。

Q: 現在，皇族と言われるのはどんな方ですか？

天皇家の一員として，結婚をして「〜宮」という称号を持つことができるのは，天皇の直系の子供に限られます。

従って，1995年末現在，皇族と言われる方々は次の通りです。天皇・皇后，皇太后，皇太子・皇太子妃，秋篠宮(あきしののみや)・秋篠宮妃とその子供，紀宮(のりのみや)。天皇のご兄弟である常陸宮(ひたちのみや)・常陸宮妃。昭和天皇のご兄弟である三笠宮(みかさのみや)・三笠宮妃，亡くなられた高松宮(たかまつのみや)のお妃。三笠宮の子息である寛仁(ともひと)親王・妃とその子供，桂宮(かつらのみや)，高円宮(たかまどのみや)・高

• Can a woman become emperor?

Recorded imperial chronologies note ten women emperors. The first was the Emperor Suiko (592–628), and the most recent was the Emperor Go-Sakuramachi (1762–70).

Although the imperial line is determined by a hereditary system whereby paternal male heirs succeed to the throne, in a few cases, when the death of a reigning emperor left no heirs who could satisfy the requirements for imperial succession, the empress, imperial princess, or the crown princess acceded to the throne.

As of October 1995, the Emperor's two sons, the Crown Prince and Prince Akishino, are in good health. However, since the Crown Prince does not yet have any children, and Prince Akishino's two children are both girls, the line of succession to the throne would be in the order of the Crown Prince, followed by Prince Akishino, Prince Hitachi (the brother of the Heisei Emperor, and Prince Mikasa (the brother of the Shōwa Emperor). However, in the event that they do not give birth to a son, it may open the possibility for an empress or a princess to the throne.

• At present, who is considered to be part of the imperial family?

The only people who as members of the imperial family can marry and hold the title *-miya* (prince or princess), are the children of the Emperor.

Accordingly, as of the end of 1995, those considered to be members of the imperial family are: the Emperor and Empress; the Empress Dowager; the Crown Prince and Princess; Prince and Princess Akishino, their children; Princess Nori; the brother of the Heisei Emperor—Prince and Princess Hitachi; the brothers of the Shōwa Emperor—Prince and Princess Mikasa, the wife of the late Prince Takamatsu; the children of

円宮妃とその子供。

皇室は「皇室典範」という法律で身分や権利・義務などを規定されておりますが，一般国民と同様に法律が適用されます。唯一異なるのは戸籍がないということです。

そして名前に必要な名字がありません。皇太子は，単に徳仁（なるひと），皇太子妃となった小和田雅子さんは，単に雅子なのです。宮家の名前が与えられたとき，それが姓の役割をします。

日本の歴史

Q: 邪馬台国はホントにあったんですか？

中国の歴史書「魏志倭人伝（ぎしわじんでん）」に，日本は2世紀後半には大いに国が乱れ，多くの国々が争っていたが，邪馬台国が卑弥呼を女王に立てたところ大乱が治まった，とあります。

邪馬台国が存在したのはまちがいないのですが，その所在地については，昔から論争の種になっています。

学説は大きくわけると2つあります。1つは邪馬台国は九州にあったとする説，もう1つは奈良県付近にあったとする説で，今でも論争が続いています。

Q: 古墳時代とはどんな時代ですか？

古墳とは当時の支配者（豪族）の墓で，形は各種あるのですが，いずれも小山のように土を盛りあげ，その表面には埴輪とよぶ土製の人物

Prince Mikasa—Prince and Princess Tomohito, their children, Prince Katsura, Prince and Princess Takamado and their children.

The status, rights, and responsibilities of the imperial family are stipulated under the Imperial Household Law, but imperial family members are also subject to the same laws governing regular citizens. The only difference is that they do not have family registers.

Also, there is no required surname for the imperial family. The name for the Crown Prince is simply Naruhito; Owada Masako, who became the Crown Princess, is simply called Masako. When an imperial family name is accorded, this serves as the surname.

Japanese History

• Did the country of Yamatai really exist?

According to "The Account of the Wa People" in the Chinese historical text *Wei zhi* (The Wei Chronicle), Japan in the latter half of the second century was undergoing much strife, with most of its countries at war, but came under control with the accession of Himiko as Queen of Yamatai.

While there is no doubt that Yamatai did exist, for a long time there has been much debate over the actual location of this country.

There are two major theories. One holds that Yamatai was located in Kyūshū, while the other claims that Yamatai was located near Nara Prefecture; the debate continues to this day.

• What was the Kofun period like?

Kofun is the name for the tombs of the rulers (*gōzoku*) of the period. While they came in various shapes, all were built of mounded earth, with clay sculptures (*haniwa*) of people and

Haniwa

や馬などを飾り，内部には遺体のほかに，武器・鏡・装身具などの副葬品をおさめる石室があります。

こうした古墳がさかんにつくられた4世紀から7世紀末を古墳時代といいます。この時代，次第に大和国家としての統一が出来上がっていきます。

7世紀はじめには聖徳太子(574–622)が，「冠位十二階制」や「憲法十七条」を制定して，国家としての基盤を作りました。

またこの時代は，中国，朝鮮からの渡来人が手工業や農業，土木技術の新技術を伝えた時代です。

Q:奈良時代とはどんな時代ですか？

奈良時代は，8世紀の大部分，710年から794年の間，現在の奈良に都が置かれていた時代です。この都を平城京と呼びます。

奈良時代には中央集権となり，律令制度が敷かれます。

日本の歴史の主な時代

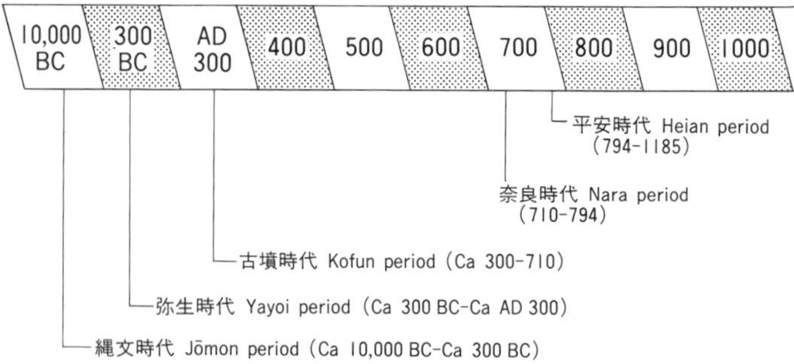

horses adorning the exterior of the tomb, and funerary goods such as weapons, mirrors, and personal ornaments enclosed with the body inside the interior stone chamber.

The Kofun Period refers to the period from the fourth century to the seventh century when these tombs were actively being built. It is during this period that gradual unification under the Yamato polity took place.

In the beginning of the seventh century, Prince Shōtoku (574–622) laid the foundations for the state by instituting the *Kan'i Jūnikai* (twelve grades of cap rank) System of courtly ranks and the Seventeen Article Constitution.

This was also the period when Chinese and Korean immigrants came to Japan and conveyed new technology in handicrafts, farming, and construction.

• What was the Nara period like?

The Nara period spans most of the 8th century, from 710 to 794, marking the years when the present-day city of Nara was the seat of the capital. This capital was called Heijōkyō.

The Nara period saw the centralization of power and the implementation of the *ritsuryō* (legal codes) system of government.

Major Periods in Japanese History

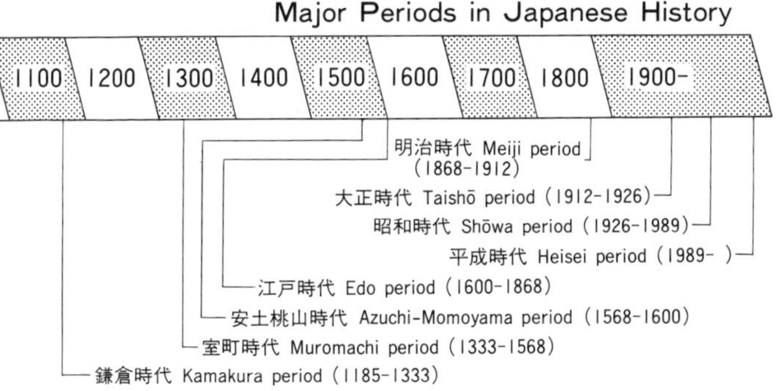

仏教は政府に保護されて，大いに栄えました。現存する銅製の仏像では世界最大の，東大寺の大仏が作られたのもこの時代です。

また，中国の唐に何度も人を派遣するなど海外との交流も盛んな時代で，唐の文化を中心に，朝鮮の文化やインド，ペルシアの文化の影響も見られる時代です。

Q: 平安時代とはどんな時代ですか？

現在の京都に都が移されたのは8世紀末のことで，こののち1000年以上，ずっと日本の都でしたが，そのうちの12世紀末までの約400年間を平安時代といいます。

奈良時代に続いて，天皇の下で貴族が実権を握って政治を行っていきますが，同時に各地域の豪族が次第に私有地を拡大し，周辺との争いから身を守るために武装して団結します。そして，ついに平氏とよばれる一族が政治の全権を握ります。やがて来る武士の時代のさきがけです。

文化の面では，唐の文化の模倣と吸収から脱して，日本の独特の風土や日本人の感性による文化へと移行しました。世界的に有名な紫式部の『源氏物語』もこの時代の作品です。

Q: 鎌倉時代とはどんな時代ですか？

平安時代末期に政治の実権を握っていた平氏も，1185年，ついに源氏に滅ぼされます。

Buddhism flourished under the protection of the state. It was during this period that the world's largest existing bronze sculpture of Buddha—the Great Buddha of Tōdaiji temple—was built.

Foreign interaction thrived during this period, with a number of embassies dispatched to Tang China. China exerted a great influence on the culture of this period, and was in turn influenced by the cultures of Korea, India and Persia.

• What was the Heian period like?

At the end of the 8th century, the capital was moved to present-day Kyōto, which remained Japan's capital for over a thousand years; the Heian period designates a span of roughly 400 years until the 12th century.

Continuing from the Nara period, aristocrats under the emperor held actual power and controlled the government, but at the same time, powerful clans from a variety of regions expanded their private landholdings, and became unified and militarized in order to protect themselves from war with neighboring regions. Eventually, the Taira clan was able to grasp full political control. It was a harbinger of the age of the warrior that was soon to follow.

In the cultural sphere, Japan was able to move away from its reliance on imitating and assimilating Tang culture and proceed to forge a culture that incorporated a distinct Japanese spirit and sensitivity. The world-renowned *Tale of Genji* written by Murasaki Shikibu was one of the works produced during this period.

• What was the Kamakura period like?

The Taira family, which had grasped political power toward the end of the Heian period, soon fell to the Minamoto family in 1185.

その後，源頼朝（みなもとのよりとも）は1192年に征夷（せいい）大将軍となり，鎌倉（神奈川県）に幕府を樹立します。武家政治の始まりです。幕府は武士の長である将軍が政務をとった軍事政権です。天皇は単なる名目的な存在でした。

しかし，源氏は3代で滅び，北条（ほうじょう）氏が権力を握り，1333年，後醍醐天皇が鎌倉幕府を倒し，天皇政治を復活するまで続きます。

文化の面では，武士らしい，力強く，剛毅で，そして写実的な仏像彫刻に名作が生まれました。

Q: 室町時代とはどんな時代ですか？

室町時代は2つに分けられます。南北朝時代と戦国時代です。

南北朝時代は，1333年に鎌倉幕府を倒し，政治を京都の朝廷に取り戻した後醍醐天皇と，これに背いて，光明天皇をかついで，1336年に京都北部に幕府を開いた足利尊氏とが対立していた時代です。

戦国時代は，1467年の応仁の乱以後，1573年に織田信長が幕府を滅ぼすまでの約100 年間です。

室町時代には，全般的には，農業生産が向上し，商業も発展し，都市が栄えました。

文化面でも水墨画，能，狂言，茶の湯，生け

In 1192, Minamoto no Yoritomo was conferred the title *seii tai shōgun* (barbarian-subduing generalissimo) and established a *bakufu* (Shogunate) government at Kamakura (in Kanagawa Prefecture). This was the beginning of warrior clan politics. *Bakufu* was the name for a military regime in which the head of the warriors, or shōgun, controlled political affairs. The emperor was simply a figurehead.

However, the Minamoto family fell into decline after three generations and the Hōjō family took over power; this continued until Emperor Go-Daigo defeated the Kamakura *bakufu* government in 1333 and effected a restoration of imperial rule.

In the cultural sphere, the period gave birth to a number of famous realistic Buddhist sculptures noted for being powerful, bold, and warrior-like.

• What was the Muromachi period like?

The Muromachi period can be devided into two periods, the Northern and Southern Courts period, and the Warring States period.

The Northern and Southern Courts period is the period which saw the conflict between Emperor Go-Daigo, who had overthrown the Kamakura *bakufu* in 1333 and restored political power to the palace in Kyōto, and Ashikaga Takauji, who set up a *bakufu* government in northern Kyōto under the Emperor Kōmyō in 1336.

The Warring States period is the 100-year period beginning with the Ōnin War in 1467 and continuing until Oda Nobunaga's defeat of the *bakufu* in 1573.

Overall, the Muromachi period saw the rise of agricultural production, the growth of commercial activity, and the development of cities.

Culturally, this period witnessed the birth of ink painting,

花などがこの時代に生まれました。

Q: 安土桃山時代とはどんな時代ですか？

Oda Nobunaga
長興寺蔵

戦国時代にライバルを次々と倒していったのが織田信長でした。しかし彼は，全国統一を目前にして家臣に殺されてしまいます。その後を引き継いだのが，やはり家臣だった豊臣秀吉でした。安土桃山時代はこの織田信長と豊臣秀吉が政権を握っていた時代です。1568年（1573年説もある）から約30年という短期間ですが，日本の封建社会を発展させた点で重要な時代です。

注目すべき政策は検地と刀狩りです。農地面積や収穫高などを調べ，年貢の量と責任者を決める検地，そして，農民から一切の武器を取りあげる刀狩りは，農民の身分を固定化し，武士の支配的地位を決定づけました。

文化は桃山文化と呼ばれ，仏教の影響が弱まり，自由で豪華な様相を呈しました。高くそびえる天守閣を持つ城郭建築や金箔にきらめく障壁画がその典型です。

Q: 江戸時代とはどんな時代ですか？

豊臣家を滅ぼし，1603年，徳川家康が江戸（東京）に幕府を開いて全国を支配した260年余が江戸時代です。

幕府の最高権力者，将軍から1万石以上の領地を得た者が大名で，その領地と支配機構を藩と言います。幕府は藩を通して全国の領

Nō and *kyōgen* theater, tea ceremony, and Japanese flower arrangement.

• What was the Azuchi-Momoyama period like?

During the Warring States period, Oda Nobunaga went on to defeat one rival after another. However, just before he could achieve unification of the country, he was killed by his own vassal. The person who succeeded him was indeed his own vassal, Toyotomi Hideyoshi. Azuchi-Momoyama covers the period when political control was held by Oda Nobunaga and Toyotomi Hideyoshi. The short, roughly thirty-year span beginning in 1568 (some say 1573) was a crucial period in terms of the development of Japan's feudal society.

The policies which deserve attention are the cadastral survey and the sword hunt. The cadastral survey, which appraised the area and productivity of agricultural land, and the sword hunt, which confiscated all weaponry held by peasants, served to establish the domination of the warrior class and entrench the status of the peasant.

In terms of culture, this period gave rise to what is known as the "Momoyama culture," which saw the weakening of Buddhist influences and the emergence of a free and sumptuous style. Typifying this culture were the building of castles with soaring towers and the creation of wall and screen paintings glittering with gold leaf.

• What was the Edo period like?

The Edo Period is the 260-year span following Tokugawa Ieyasu's defeat of Toyotomi family and the establishment of a *bakufu* government in Edo (now Tōkyō) in 1603.

The *daimyō* ranged from the *Shōgun*, who sat at the apex of power, to lords controlling land worth over 10,000 *koku* (unit of measure based on rice production), and their domains

Tokugawa Ieyasu

土と民衆を支配します。この支配体制が幕藩制です。

武士をいちばん上の階級とする士農工商の制度で身分差別を強め，対外的には，鎖国政策をとり，キリスト教を禁じた時代でもあります。

しかし，国内の作物の栽培は進み，漁業も発達し，商人が力をつけて，貨幣経済が発展しました。

文化の面では，17世紀末～18世紀初めに元禄文化が花開きます。町民が担い手で，人形浄瑠璃や歌舞伎が人気を博し，松尾芭蕉が俳句を大成しました。浮世絵が創始され，のちに歌麿，北斎，広重らにひきつがれます。

明治から現代へ

Q：明治時代はどうやって誕生したのですか？

Commodore Perry

1853年，ペリー率いるアメリカ軍艦が浦賀沖に現れ開国を迫るや，国内は開国か尊皇攘夷かを巡って大混乱に陥りました。

倒幕の主力となった薩摩藩（鹿児島県）と長州藩（山口県）も，当初は尊皇攘夷でしたが，欧米の力を知るに至って開国へと方向転換します。

and the power structure imposed on them were known as *han*. The *bakufu* controlled the land and the people of the nation through these *han* units. This system of government is known as the *bakuhan* system.

This period also saw the reinforcement of a status system known as *shi-nō-kō-shō* (warrior-peasant-artisan-merchant) which placed the warrior in the top social class, and externally, the establishment of a policy of national seclusion and the prohibition of Christianity.

However, during this period, advances were made in domestic agricultural production as well as in fishing industries, which strengthened the merchant class and gave rise to a monetary economy.

Culturally, this period saw the flourishing in the latter 17th and early 18th centuries of what is known as the Genroku Era. Fostered by the townspeople, arts such as the puppet theater and *kabuki* gained much popularity, while Matsuo Bashō produced masterpieces in the *haiku* poetic form. The art of *ukiyo-e* prints also began during this period, which was later fostered by the likes of Utamaro, Hokusai, and Hiroshige.

From Meiji to the Present

• What gave birth to the Meiji period?

In 1853, Commodore Perry and his squadron of American ships appeared in Uraga Bay and pressed for the opening of the country, leaving in their wake a domestic crisis over whether to open up the country or "revere the emperor and expel the barbarians."

Even Satsuma (now Kagoshima Prefecture) and Chōshū provinces (now Yamaguchi Prefecture), which eventually overthrew the *bakufu*, initially supported the move to "revere the emperor and expel the barbarians," but eventually, with their

一方，民衆は物価上昇に苦しみ，富裕な商店を襲う打ち壊しや一揆が各地で続発，ここからも幕藩制の根底が揺るぎました。ついに15代将軍，徳川慶喜(よしのぶ)は，1867年，政権を朝廷に返します。そして天皇中心の政府を樹立する王政復古の大号令が出され，長い封建制度は終わりを告げます。明治時代の誕生です。

Q：明治時代とはどんな時代ですか？

Emperor Meiji

徳川氏から朝廷へと政権が移行し，幕府と藩による政治から国家統一へと向かうことになりました。経済は資本主義制度へと移行して，近代日本の制度ができた時代です。

1889年，明治憲法（大日本帝国憲法）が施行されて，国の政治形態の基本ができますが，「天皇は神聖にして侵すべからず」という条項があり，天皇は神格化され，日本は次第に国家主義で統一されていきます。

人民の自由と権利を伸ばすことを主張する自由民権運動も起こりますが，結局は，国家主義の名のもとに，国益が優先され，朝鮮半島，中国大陸への進出をします。

そして，これに反対する諸外国との軋轢(あつれき)も強まり，明治時代だけで，日清戦争（1894–1895），日露戦争（1904–1905）に突入し，1910年には韓

growing knowledge of the Western powers, they decided to switch their allegiance toward the drive to open up the country.

On the one hand, the masses were suffering under inflation, and riots and attacks on shops of wealthy merchants occurred in various regions, weakening the foundations of the *bakuhan* system. This led in 1867 to the relinquishment of power by the 15th Tokugawa *shōgun*, Yoshinobu, to the imperial court. A decree was made which established a government centered on the emperor, bringing to a close the long years under the feudal system. Thus the Meiji period came into being.

• What was the Meiji period like?

This period saw the transfer of power from Tokugawa to the imperial court, and the transition from a system of government based on the *bakufu* and *han* domains to a unified state. This is also the period witnessing the transition to a capitalist economy and the establishment of a modern Japanese state system.

In 1889, the Meiji Constitution (The Constitution of Imperial Japan) was promulgated, laying the foundations for the political structure of the state. It contained a clause maintaining the divinity of the emperor, claiming that the country "must not violate the sanctity of the emperor," and so Japan gradually came to be unified under the force of nationalism.

Although human rights movements took place which attempted to assert and extend the rights and freedom of citizens. In the end, under the banner of nationalism, Japan let state interests take precedence and advanced into the Korean peninsula and the Chinese continent.

Friction increased with other countries which came to oppose Japan's advances, and in the Meiji period alone, Japan entered into the Sino-Japanese War (1894–5) and the Russo-

国を日本に併合するという事態になっていきました。

Q: 大正時代とはどんな時代ですか？

Emperor Taishō

この時代は1912年から26年までの14年間という短い期間ですが，明治時代の藩閥・官僚政治による国家権力の増大に反発して，民主主義的な改革運動が起こった時代です。

憲法にのっとった政治を守ること，誰でもが選挙権を持つことができる普通選挙を求める運動などが繰り広げられます。

米騒動や労働争議も起こり，民本主義，自由主義，社会主義の運動が高まった時代です。

しかしこの「大正デモクラシー」の運動も，結局，高まる国家主義の動きに抗することはできず，日本は次第に軍国主義の国になっていきます。

Q: 昭和時代とはどんな時代ですか？

昭和を簡単に説明するのは困難です。太平洋戦争の敗戦の1945年の前と後では，根本的な違いがあるからです。

日露戦争後，日本は満州における権益の確保政策を続け，大陸に駐留する関東軍は満州占領を進めて，1932年には「満州建国宣言」をします。

国際連盟はこれに調査団を送り，日本は国際連盟を脱退します。

さらに1937年，盧溝橋(ろこうきょう)事件を契機に中国との間に戦争となり，ついには，東南アジア一帯に

Japanese War (1904–5), and went on to annex Korea in 1910.

• What was the Taishō period like?

This was a short 14-year period from 1912 to 1926, which saw the rise of democratic reform movements in opposition to growing state power in the hands of the *han* bureaucratic clique from the Meiji Period.

There was a spread of popular movements which demanded that government abide by the constitution and called for common elections which extended voting rights to all citizens.

This was a period when rice riots and labor disputes occurred, and democratic and socialist movements were heightened.

However, even this "Taishō Democracy" movement in the end could not stem rising nationalism, and Japan would increasingly turn into a militarist state.

• What was the Shōwa period like?

It is difficult to explain succinctly the Shōwa period because of the fundamental difference between the pre-World War II period before Japan's defeat in 1945 and the postwar period after 1945.

After the Russo-Japanese War, Japan continued its policy of extending its power in Manchuria, and the Kwantung Army stationed in the continent furthered its occupation of Manchuria, and in 1932 issued "Declaration of the Founding of Manchukuo."

The League of Nations sent an investigative commission to Manchuria, while Japan withdrew from the League.

In 1937, propelled by the Marco Polo Bridge Incident, Japan entered into a war with China and soon it intervened in

Emperor Shōwa and General MacArthur

も日本が介入するにおよび，1941年12月8日の真珠湾攻撃を開始の合図に，日本はアメリカその他の国々との全面戦争に突入しました。

結果は，1945年8月，敗戦。

1945年以降，占領軍の駐留の下で，日本が民主主義国家の仲間入りしていくことになりました。そして，様々な矛盾もはらみながら，日本人の勤勉さと知恵で獲得した優れた技術力で，世界の経済大国と言われるようになっていきました。

all of Southeast Asia. Japan's attack on Pearl Harbor on December 8, 1941 signalled its thrust into full-scale war with the U.S. and other countries.

In the end, Japan was defeated in August 1945.

Following 1945, under the Occupation by the Allied Forces, Japan gradually came to be accepted into the community of democratic nations. And, while confronting numerous dilemmas, Japan gained recognition as a global economic superpower through its superior technological prowess, which was achieved by the ingenuity and diligence of the Japanese people.

3

日本の政治と経済

日本の憲法

Q: 日本の現憲法は，いつ，どのようにして作られたのですか？

1945年8月の太平洋戦争後，日本を占領下に置いた連合国総司令部（GHQ）から憲法改正の勧告を受けて，日本政府は翌1946年1月に改正案を作成しました。その内容は旧大日本帝国憲法の影を濃厚に残したもので，国民の権利は拡張されましたが，国の主権は天皇にあるままとしていました。

そこで連合国最高司令官マッカーサーはこれを拒否し，2月13日に別の憲法試案，いわゆるマッカーサー草案を提示し，日本政府にこの検討を求めました。

日本政府はこの草案をもとに3月6日に新憲法をまとめ，1947年5月3日に，現在の日本国憲法が施行されることになったのです。

日本の保守層の中には，この憲法は自分た

3

GOVERNMENT AND ECONOMY

Constitution of Japan

• When and how was the Japanese Constitution made?

As suggested by the General Headquarters of the Allied Forces occupying Japan after the World War II, the Japanese government completed a draft of the revision of the Meiji Constitution in January 1946. In this draft, with no major changes from the original constitution, it was defined that the sovereignty rest with the Emperor, although the people's rights were extended significantly.

General MacArthur rejected this draft, and presented the so-called "MacArthur draft" on February 13, for the Japanese government's consideration.

The government drew up a new constitution based on the MacArthur draft on March 6, and it came into force on May 3, 1947.

Some conservatives in Japan have criticized this new con-

ちで手に入れたものというよりも「与えられた憲法」だとして，批判の声を上げる人もいます。

Q：いつも問題になる憲法第2章第9条とはどんな内容ですか？

第9条の全文を挙げてみましょう。

「日本国民は，正義と秩序を基調とする国際平和を誠実に希求し，国権の発動たる戦争と，武力による威嚇又は武力の行使は，国際紛争を解決する手段としては，永久にこれを放棄する。

前項の目的を達するため，陸海空軍その他の戦力は，これを保持しない。国の交戦権は，これを認めない。」

素直に読めば，いかなる軍備も持たないと読むことができます。しかし，この条項には自衛権は含まれない，とする日本の保守勢力の主張に押されて，1954年に自衛隊が誕生しました。

Q：憲法はどのようにしたら改定できるのですか？

憲法を改正するためには，衆議院，参議院，それぞれ総議員の3分の2以上の賛成で発議され，それを国民投票にかけて，過半数の賛成を必要とします。しかし，1947年の現憲法の施行以来，現在まで一度も憲法改正のための国民投票が行われたことはありません。

stitution because it was something given to the people, rather than something they acquired by themselves.

• What is the content of Article 9, Chapter 2 of the Constitution, which is said to be most controversial?

Article 9, Chapter 2 of the Japanese Constitution translates as follows:

"Aspiring sincerely to an international peace based on justice and order, the Japanese people forever renounce war as a sovereign right of the nation and the threat or use of force as a means of settling international disputes.

In order to accomplish the aim of the preceding paragraph, land, sea, and air forces, as well as other war potential, will never be maintained. The right of belligerency of the state will not be recognized."

The article, when interpreted straightforwardly, means that Japan can never possess any type of military forces. However, the Self Defense Force came into existence in 1954, supported by conservatives who insisted that the right of self defense is not implied in the article.

• How can the Constitution be amended?

Amendment to the Constitution first requires an approval of more than two thirds of the members of the House of Representatives, and the House of Councilors respectively, and then an approval of the majority of the people of Japan by a national referendum. However, since the promulgation of the present Constitution in 1947, no national referendum for its amendment has been conducted.

政治の仕組み

Q: 日本の議会はどういう構成になっていますか？

The House of Representatives

日本の議会は Diet と表現され，衆議院と参議院の2院で構成されています。

両院とも国民を代表する議員で構成されています。国民の意思を代表するのが衆議院，衆議院の判断の不備や行き過ぎを是正する役目をするのが参議院です。

Q: 議員は何人いて，どうやって選ぶのですか？

Streetside campaigning for an election

衆議院は500人，参議院は252人が定員です。

衆議院に関しては，大激論の末，1994年に選挙法が改正され，小選挙区比例代表制が採択されてこの数字になっています。

衆議院の選挙制度は2つの投票方法によっています。500人の内300人は小選挙区制，つまり全国を300に分けた区域の中からそれぞれ1名が選ばれます。

そして残りの200人には比例代表制が適用されます。この制度では，全国を11のブロックに分けて選挙区とし，投票は候補者ではなく，政党に対して行います。政党に対する投票で各政党が全国で得た数に比例して，議席を配分します。

有権者は小選挙区で候補者を1人，比例選挙区で政党を1つ選んで投票することになります。

Government System

• What is the parliament system of Japan like?

The parliament of Japan is called the 'Diet', which is made up of the House of Representatives and the House of Councilors.

Both of them consist of elected members representing the nation. The House of Representatives is to mainly represent the people's opinions, and the House of Councilors is to check the power and judgement of the House of Representatives.

• How many members of parliament are there and how are they elected?

The House of Representatives has 500 members and the House of Councilors has 252.

The number in the House of Representatives reflects the recent revision of the election law, which, after heated discussions, was enacted in 1994.

The election system for the House of Representatives consists of two voting methods. Of the 500 seats, 300 are elected according to the "small electoral district system," in which one candidate is elected for each of the 300 districts of the country.

And the "proportional representative system" is applied to the remaining 200 seats. In this system, the country is divided into 11-block electoral districts, and votes are cast for political parties instead of candidates. The seats for members of parliament are allocated to each party in proportion to the number of votes gained nationwide.

Therefore, a voter casts a ballot for one candidate in the small electoral district, and a ballot for one party in the proportional electoral district.

参議院は，100人を比例代表制で選び，残りの152人を都道府県を単位とした選挙区から選出します。

Q: 日本の政治の仕組みはどうなっていますか？

日本の政治体制は多くの民主国家同様，立法，司法，行政で成り立っています。それぞれの権力分野は独立しています。国会が立法権を，内閣が行政権を，裁判所が司法権を持っています。

そして，実際の政治は国会が内閣を組織するという「議院内閣制」によって行われています。首相は議会の議決で選任され，大臣は首相が選任します。

しかし，アメリカのような他の民主主義国家と違って，大臣は議員の中から選任されることが多いので，立法府と行政府の境界線があいまいになるという現実があります。

Q: 首相はどのようにして選ばれるのですか？

日本の首相は国会の議決で決まりますが，だれでも首相に立候補できるかというと，そういうわけにはいきません。

日本の政治は政党政治です。そして首相の資格は国会議員であること，および文民であることが条件です。日本では正式の軍隊はありませんので，誰もが文民ですが……

政党は勢力拡張をねらい，それぞれに，また連立して自分たちの党の党首，リーダーを首相の座に推します。

A hundred members of the House of Councilors are elected according to the "proportional representative system" and the remaining 152 members are elected from electoral districts based on municipalities.

• What is the government system of Japan like?

The Japanese government, as in many democratic countries, is composed of a legislative branch, an administrative branch and a judiciary branch. Each of the branches is independent of the others in terms of its powers. The Diet is vested with legislative powers, the cabinet with administrative powers, and the court with judiciary powers.

The execution of administrative powers is based on the "parliamentary cabinet system," in which the cabinet is organized by the Diet. The prime minister is designated by the Diet and the state ministers are chosen by the Prime Minister.

However, unlike in some of the democratic countries such as the United States, the majority of the state ministers are chosen from members of the Diet, which can obscure the line between the legislature and the administration.

• How is the Prime Minister elected?

The Japanese Prime Minister is decided by the Diet, but not everyone can run for Prime Minister.

Because of the nature of the Japanese government which is party-based, candidates for the prime minister must be members of the Diet. And he or she must be a civilian (Actually, all Japanese are civilians since there exists no formal military in Japan).

Political parties, independent and coalition alike, recommend the presidents or leaders of their parties for the position of Prime Minister, in hopes of increasing their power.

そのために政党間の権力闘争が激しく渦巻き，国民の利益よりも自分たちの利益に走ることになりかねません。いつも金権政治の駆け引きになる恐れがあるのです。日本で政治が遠いものに感じられるのは，この首相の選び方にあるのかもしれません。

Q: 日本にはどんな政党がありますか？

1990年代に入ってから政界の再編成が進んでおり，自由民主党の分裂，社会党の衰退，公明党の変身など，大変流動的な状態で，21世紀に入るまでは変動が続くのではないかと言われています。

一応，1996年の2月の段階で，衆参国会に議席を持つ政党は，次の通りです。

自由民主党
社会民主党
新進党
新党さきがけ
日本共産党
公明党

Q: 大臣は何人いるのですか？

大臣の選任は内閣総理大臣の権限ですが，次の決まりがあります。

1) 内閣総理大臣以外の国務大臣は，総員20人以内。
2) 文民でなくてはならない。
3) 過半数が国会議員でなくてはならない。

The fight for power among parties is so severe that emphasis is often placed on their self interest rather than on the interests of the people. There is always a fear of money politics being the name of the game. The fact that most people in Japan feel somewhat isolated from actual politics may stem from the way the Prime Minister is chosen.

• What political parties are there in Japan?

Since the beginning of the 1990's, the political climate of Japan has been quite volatile. The division of the Liberal Democratic Party, the decline of the Social Democratic Party, and the transformation of the Kōmei Party have caused a chaotic situation, which is expected to continue until the turn of the century.

The parties which have seats in the Diet as of February 1996 are:

The Liberal Democratic Party
The Social Democratic Party
The New Frontier Party
The New Party Sakigake
The Japanese Communist Party
Kōmei

• How many ministers are there in the Cabinet?

The Prime Minister has the power to choose state ministers, and the following are the qualifications they must satisfy.

1) The number of state ministers excluding the Prime Minister must be less than 20.
2) State ministers must be civilians.
3) The majority of the state ministers are to be chosen from Diet members.

上記の決まりですが，これまでの例としていつも目一杯の20人がなり，しかも国会議員以外の人が大臣になるのは，毎回，せいぜい1人か2人というのが慣例です。

国会議員のだれもが大臣になりたがるのは本音で,「大臣病」という言葉があるほどです。

現在大臣と称される職務は，総理大臣の他に次の通りです。

外務大臣，大蔵大臣，通産大臣，法務大臣，郵政大臣，文部大臣，運輸大臣，建設大臣，農林水産大臣，厚生大臣，労働大臣，自治大臣，防衛庁長官，総務庁長官，北海道・沖縄開発庁長官，経済企画庁長官，科学技術庁長官，環境庁長官，国土庁長官，そして官房長官。

Q: 日本の「官僚」はどうして優秀と言われるのですか?

首相が代われば各省庁の大臣も代わりますが，通常，官僚は終身雇用でそれぞれの省庁に雇われていますから，自ずとその道の専門家となっていきます。

問題は，各省庁の役人がそれぞれ自分たちの職務に忠実なあまり「縄張り意識」に陥ることです。その結果「縦割り行政」となり，各省庁間の密接な結びつきを失っています。このような

So far, a maximum of 20 ministers are chosen and the vast majority of them almost always have been members of the Diet, with only 1 or 2 at a time selected from outside the Diet.

Virtually every member of the Diet has an ambition to become a state minister, and there is even a term called "minister disease."

The following are the state minister positions of Japan (excluding the Prime Minister): Minister of Foreign Affairs; Minister of Finance; Minister of International Trade and Industry; Minister of Justice; Minister of Post and Telecommunications; Minister of Education, Culture and Science; Minister of Transport; Minister of Construction; Minister of Agriculture, Forestry and Fisheries; Minister of Health and Welfare; Minister of Labor; Minister of Home Affairs; Director General of the Defense Agency; Director General of the Management and Coordination Agency; Director General of the Hokkaido/Okinawa Development Agency; Director General of the Economic Planning Agency; Director General of the Science and Technology; Director General of the Environment Agency; Director General of the National Land Agency; and the Chief Cabinet Secretary.

• Why are Japanese bureaucrats said to be so competent?

In comparison with ministers who change their job every time the Prime Minister changes, bureaucrats normally work for one ministry or agency on a lifetime employment basis, which means they have enough time to develop their expertise in certain areas.

The problem is that some officials are so dedicated to their duties that they fall in a pit of being territorial about their job. This results in what is called "vertically-split administration," which lacks close-knit relations between each ministry and

お役所主義では，1か所で決めればいいことを，あちらこちらの省庁の許可が必要になるということになります。そこで，効率よく柔軟性のある「行政改革」が日本の将来の大きな課題の1つです。

Q:首都東京は，いつ，どのようにして決められたのですか?

1867年，明治維新で徳川幕府が倒され，1868年の明治政府の誕生と共に，それまで徳川幕府の城下町であった江戸を，引き続き新政府の拠点とすることにし，名前を江戸から東京と改めたものです。「東の京」ということからの命名です。

Q:日本の地方行政はどのように行われていますか?

日本は憲法で地方自治が保障されています。従って，都道府県の知事，区長，市長，村長や議会の議員を選挙で選び，それぞれの地域の行政を任せます。

しかし，地方公共団体の事務の大半は，国から委託された行政事務であり，また，財政面では，地方の税金だけでは地域の公共事業の遂行は困難ですので，国への依存度が非常に高いのが現実です。

Q:都，道，府，県はどう違うのですか?

歴史的な経過による呼び方の違いだけで，地方自治法上は全く同じです。

都は東京都だけに用いられ，道(どう)は北海道だけに用いられます。府がつけられるのは2つあ

agency. In this type of red tape, it is common that something is decided after it is sent from one office to another, even if it is not necessary to do so. It is Japan's task for the future to implement administrative reform while encouraging efficiency and flexibility.

• When and how was Tōkyō designated as the capital of Japan?

The Tokugawa shogunate (feudal government) turned its power to the Emperor in 1867, and in 1868 the new government was formed with Emperor Meiji (Meiji Restoration). Edo, the castle town of the feudal government, was designated as the base of the new government and its name was changed to Tōkyō. Tōkyō literally means "eastern capital."

• How is the local government of Japan conducted?

The Constitution of Japan guarantees local autonomy. Governors, ward chiefs, city mayors, village mayors and members of the assembly are directly elected by residents.

However, the municipalities are heavily dependent on the state, because their major job is business entrusted by the state, and public works in those municipalities cannot be implemented without financial assistance from the State.

• How are *to*, *dō*, *fu*, *ken* different?

The difference is simply a matter of their historical backgrounds; they are all defined in the same manner under local autonomy law.

To is used exclusively for Tōkyō, as in Tōkyō-to (Tōkyō Metropolis), and *dō* is used only for Hokkai-dō. There are two

って，大阪府と京都府です。県は43あります。

経済・産業・貿易

Q: 日本経済が強かった理由は何ですか？

日本の経済が伸びた理由は，東西冷戦のおかげと言われます。アメリカとソ連を始め，冷戦の影におびえる各国が，軍備に予算をとられている間に，平和憲法の下で，日本は経済のみに集中できたのです。

貿易依存度という指標があります。貿易額（輸入額＋輸出額）を国民所得で割ったもので，その貿易の活発さを表します。

日本の貿易依存度は，1955年では10%でしたが，1970年には20%を超えています。1985年以降も22–23%を維持しています。

世界各国の中で，このように伸びたのは日本だけで，強力な工業生産力と輸出力がこれを支えました。1980年代半ばの日本の急速な経済発展は，世界に脅威を与えてきました。

国民総生産も，1960年には日本は世界の国民総生産の2.8%を占めていただけですが，1980年には 10.1%という急激な伸びを示したのです。

日本経済は1980年後半まで順調な伸びを示します。その後，いわゆるバブル経済という，かつてない土地と株価の急上昇が，3年にわたって日本を襲います。

municipalities with *fu* attached to them, which are Ōsaka-fu and Kyōto-fu, and there are 43 *ken*, usually translated as prefecture.

Economy, Industry and Trade

• What is the reason for Japan's economic strength?

A contributing factor to the growth of Japan's economy is said to have been the cold war threat. While many countries including the United States and the former Soviet Union had to allot a tremendous amount of money to their armaments after World War II, Japan under the peace Constitution was able to concentrate its efforts on the economy.

One of the indices that measures the vitality of a country's trade economy is the so-called "degree of dependence on foreign trade." It is a ratio of the total amount of trade (imports and exports) to the national income.

Japan's degree of dependence on foreign trade was 10% in 1955, and exceeded 20% in 1970. It has been steady at 22 to 23% since 1985.

Among the countries in the world, only Japan has experienced such an increase in trade, which has been supported by competitive industrial production and strong exports. Japan's rapid economic growth until the mid 80's was a matter of amazement to the world.

As far as the Gross National Product is concerned, Japan's GNP was only 2.8% of the world's GNP in 1960, but it grew rapidly to 10.1% in 1980.

Japan's economy showed steady growth till the late 80's. Then a period of unprecedented asset and stock price inflation, called the "bubble economy," swept across the nation for about three years.

しかし，1991年には，株価と土地の急落と共にバブルははじけて，日本は深刻な景気後退に見舞われ始めました。

Q: 日本経済の伸びは不景気で止まったのでしょうか？

次の表は日本，アメリカ，EUの1992–95年の実質経済成長率です。1991年4月から始まった不況の姿がこの数字に現れています。

	1992	1993	1994	1995
日本	1.1	0.1	1.0	2.5
アメリカ	2.3	3.1	3.9	3.1
EU	1.1	-0.3	2.5	3.2

（OECD，"Economic Outlook" (1994)による。1995年は予測）

不景気はすでに底をついて，1995年から回復に向かうという予測になっていますが，現在も，日本が大きな課題に面してることは否定できません。

円高が大きな問題です。1993年に1ドル120円台であった円が，1995年には約80円を記録することもあった円高や，世界から米などあらゆる分野での輸入規制の撤廃を迫られるなどして，日本は国際的な競争力を失いつつあります。

21世紀までに，日本の経済を引っ張っていく産業（リーディング産業）が誕生する可能性があるかどうかなど，難しい課題が山積みです。

In 1991, when the "bubble" burst with the plunge of stock and land prices, Japan's economy started experiencing a serious recession.

• Has the growth of Japan's economy stopped because of the recession?

The chart below shows the economic growth rate of Japan, the United States and the European Union between 1992 and 1995. It indicates how seriously Japan has been affected by the recession, which began in April 1991.

	1992	1993	1994	1995
Japan	1.1	0.1	1.0	2.5
the United States	2.3	3.1	3.9	3.1
EU	1.1	-0.3	2.5	3.2

(OECD, *Economic Outlook*, 1994. The numbers for 1995 are estimates.)

Although the recession is said to have reached its bottom and the economy as a whole is expected to start recovering in 1995, there is no denying that Japan is currently confronted with a great challenge.

The appreciation of the yen is a big issue. In 1993 the exchange rate hovered at around 120 yen against the dollar, but there were certain points in 1995 that it marked a high record of about 80 yen. In addition, Japan has been urged by other countries to eliminate import restrictions on various items including rice. Due to such problems, Japan seems to be losing its competitive edge in international trade.

There are a mountain of difficult issues that Japan has to face, for example, whether or not a leading industry that boosts the economy will be born by the beginning of the 21st century.

Q: 対米黒字が減らないのはどうしてですか？

日本の貿易黒字は長い間，米国から非難を受けています。1970年代は，繊維製品，カラーテレビ，工業機械，1980年代は自動車，半導体，VTR などが日本優位で，対米黒字が減らないとアメリカからの非難を受けてきました。1990年代には，日本の経済構造自体に問題あり，という主張も出てきています。

現在は，1993年7月に設置された日米新経済協議のもとに，経常黒字縮小とアメリカの財政赤字削減を目指す「マクロ経済政策」，個別の製品を取り上げる「分野別の協議」，そして，日米だけでなく「地球的協力分野」の3つの観点から協議が進んでいます。

Q: 日本が外国にいちばん強い製品は何ですか？

Shipping of cars

この答えは日本の製品の輸出依存度を見てみると明解です。輸出依存度というのは，生産数量に対する輸出数量の割合です。

1993年の数字です。

1位	時計	85.7%
2位	船舶	82.9%
3位	カメラ	81.6%
4位	ビデオ	72.9%
5位	工作機械	50.1%
6位	自動車	46.0%
7位	合成繊維	46.0%

（通商白書，1994）

上記の製品は，世界の市場に広く受け入れ

• Why hasn't Japan's trade surplus against the United States been reduced?

Japan's trade surplus has long been criticized by the United States. In the 1970's, textile products, color TV sets, and industrial machinery were the targets of criticism, while in the 80's, the targets of criticism were automobiles, semiconductors and VTRs. In the 90's, the criticism turns to Japan's economic structure itself, saying it has been the major cause of the trade surplus problem.

Currently, negotiations are taking place between the two countries based on the US-Japan Framework Talks on Bilateral Trade launched in July 1993. The talks focus on the following three areas: reduction of Japan's trade surplus as well as the U.S. financial deficit, negotiations concerning each product, and global cooperation.

• What Japanese products are dominant in trade with foreign countries?

The answer to the question lies in the "degree of dependence on exports" which means the ratio of exports to the amount of production, of Japanese products.

The following are the figures for 1993.

1. watches and clocks	85.7%
2. vessels	82.9%
3. cameras	81.6%
4. VCRs	72.9%
5. machine tools	50.1%
6. automobiles	46.0%
7. synthetic fiber	46.0%

(*MITI White Paper*, 1994)

The above listed products have been widely accepted in

られており、製品の質が圧倒的によく，価格の上でも競争に負けません。

Q: 日本は何をいちばんたくさん輸入していますか？

1993年の輸入依存度を見るとすぐに分かります，次の表は国内消費のうち，主に輸入に頼っている品の順位です。

1位	鉄鉱石	100.0%
1位	ニッケル	100.0%
3位	銅鉱	99.7%
4位	原油	99.6%
5位	小麦	90.1%
6位	塩	84.5%
7位	液化石油ガス	76.8%
8位	木材	75.4%

輸出入品目の構成(1994年)

輸出 Export

- 0.5% 食料品 Foodstuffs
  - 0.2% 魚介類 Fish and shellfish
- 2.1% 繊維品 Textile products
  - 0.5% 合成繊維織物 Synthetic fiber textiles
- 6.0% 化学品 Chemical products
  - 2.0% 有機化合物 Organic compounds
  - 1.7% プラスチック Plastics
- 6.1% 金属品 Metal products
  - 3.8% 鉄鋼 Iron and steel
  - 1.6% 金属製品 Metal products
- 76.0% 機械機器 Machinery and equipment
  - 14.4% 自動車 Automobiles
  - 7.4% 電子部品など Electronic parts, etc.
  - 4.0% コンピューター Computers
  - 4.0% 光学機器など Optical equipment, etc.
  - 2.9% 船舶 Ships
  - 2.2% 通信機器 Communications equipment
  - 1.2% 金属加工機械 Metal-working machinery
- 1.2% 非金属鉱物製品 Non-metal, mineral products
- 8.0% その他 Others

the world market because of their high quality and competitive prices.

• What does Japan import most?

The "degree of dependence on imports" in 1993 provides the answer to the question. The following is the ranking of items where domestic consumption is mainly dependent on imports.

1. iron ore	100.0%
1. nickel	100.0%
3. copper ore	99.7%
4. crude oil	99.6%
5. flour	90.1%
6. salt	84.5%
7. LPG (liquefied petroleum gas)	76.8%
8. lumber	75.4%

The Composition of Japan's Export and Import Goods, 1994

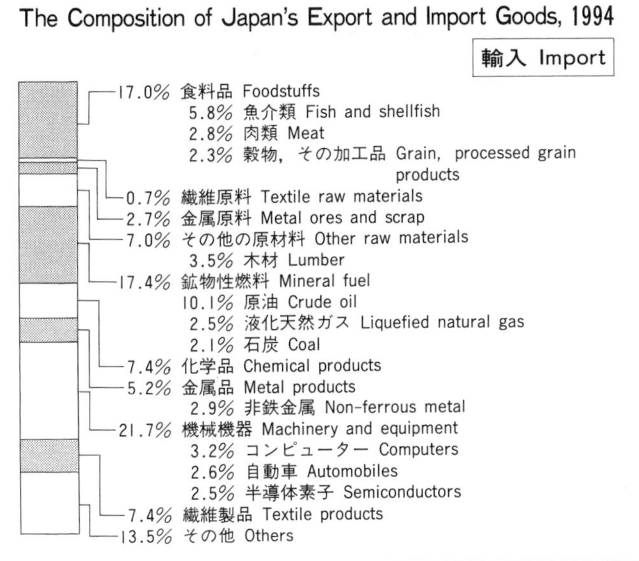

この数字と，前の質問の「日本が外国に対していちばん強い製品は何ですか？」の輸出依存度の数字を見ていますと，日本の経済がいわゆる加工貿易で，エネルギーや工業原料の多くを輸入し，加工して製品を輸出することによって成り立っているという姿が浮き彫りになってきます。

Q: 日本は自給自足ができますか？

他の先進国と比べても，はるかに日本は輸入食料に依存しています。主要な国の輸入総額の中で，食料・飲料と燃料の輸入の割合を見てみましょう。

	食料・飲料	燃料
日本	16.0%	22.6%
アメリカ	5.5%	10.6%
ドイツ	9.6%	7.5%
フランス	10.1%	8.6%
イギリス	10.7%	5.6%
イタリア	11.8%	8.5%

（国連貿易統計年鑑，1992年）

日本は食料だけでなく，燃料や，何かを生産するためのエネルギー源も他の国に頼らねばなりません。いざ，耕地を増やして何か農作物を作ろうとしても，元の農地は宅地に売られて，耕作できる土地はほとんどなくなってしまっており，不可能なのです。

Q: 日本の農業は，戦後，どのように変わってきたのですか？

1960年には，農業に従事する人の人数は，総就業人口の26.8%でしたが，1992年には，なんと，5.5%にまで減っています。耕地面積も，

Compare the figures shown above with those of the degree of dependence on exports in answer to the previous question. This brings out the fact that Japan's trade consists of what is called "improvement trade," in which it sustains itself by importing energy sources and raw materials, processing them into products, and exporting them to the world.

• Can Japan be self sufficient?

Compared with other developed countries, Japan is far more dependent on imported foodstuffs. The following chart indicates the ratio of imported provisions, beverages and fuels to the total imports of major developed countries.

	Provisions & Beverages	Fuels
Japan	16.0%	22.6%
the United States	5.5%	10.6%
Germany	9.6%	7.5%
France	10.1%	8.6%
the United Kingdom	10.7%	5.6%
Italy	11.8%	8.5%

(*UN Yearbook of International Trade Statistics*, 1992)

Japan must depend on other countries in terms of not only foodstuffs but also fuel, or sources of energy for production. Promoting farming by increasing arable land is almost impossible because a large part of former agricultural land has been turned into housing land, and there is very little land left to be cultivated.

• How has Japan's agriculture developed since World War II?

The number of people engaged in agriculture was 26.8% of the working population in 1960, but it dropped to as low as 5.5% by 1992. The arable land area was also reduced by 20%.

20%も減少しています。

Reaping rice

しかし，品種の改良と栽培技術の向上，化学肥料と農薬の大量使用，農作業の機械化によって，個々の作物の耕地単位当たりの収穫量は大幅に伸びました。

一方，政府は，戦後の農業の振興のために，食糧管理制度，牛肉や砂糖など各種の価格安定法などの保護政策をとってきましたが，そのため，国際競争力がなくなってしまいました。

現実に，生産効率が悪く，輸入価格に対抗できない農産物は淘汰され，日本の食用農産物の自給率は激減しているのです。

1992年まで自給率が100%であった米でさえ，1993年には75%（概算）と言われます。果実でさえ，1960年は100%であったものが，1993年は54%だそうです。小麦は10%，大豆はなんと2%だけです。もはや日本は食料の自給自足は不可能な国になっています。

Q：水産国ニッポンにとって，今，何がいちばんの課題ですか？

Tsukiji wholesale market

日本はアイスランドに次いで，1人当たりの魚介類の消費量が多い国ですが，漁獲量は，1989年以降，減り続けています。

かつては水産王国日本として，世界一の漁業生産を誇っていましたが，1989年には中国に抜かれました。

1992年度の漁業生産は927万トンで，世界の生産量の8.9%を占めていますが，それでは国内消費をまかなえず，37.4%を輸入に頼っています。

国際的な200カイリ漁業専管水域の設定によ

However, productivity showed substantial growth due to improvements in breeding, cultivation technology, utilization of chemical fertilizer and insecticide, and automation of production processes.

The post-war government took measures to protect the farmer by enforcing the Food Law and price control laws for produce such as beef and sugar, which resulted in a loss of international competitiveness for Japanese farm produce.

Consequently, produce with lower production efficiency have been weeded out in competition with imported produce, and the self-sufficiency rate of Japan has dropped dramatically.

The self-sufficiency rate of rice, which was 100% in 1992, dwindled to 75% in 1993. The rate for fruits was reduced to 54% in 1993 from 100% in 1960. Only 10% of flour and 2% of soybeans are produced domestically. This shows that it is virtually impossible for Japan to feed itself without depending on imports.

- **At present, what is the biggest problem for the fishery industry in Japan?**

Japan consumes the second largest amount of seafood in the world after Iceland, but its haul has been on the decline since 1989.

Japan boasted of the world's largest fishery yield for many years until 1989, when China took over first place.

The yield in 1992 was 9.27 million tons, which was 8.9% of the world yield, but that does not meet the needs of this fish-eating nation. About 37.4% of the fish consumed is imported.

With the 200-mile fishery zone restricting deep-sea fish-

り，日本が得意としていた遠洋漁業の道がせばめられた今，栽培漁業を振興する以外に道がありません。

Q: 工業国ニッポンの21世紀の見通しは？

日本の工業は戦後，鉄鋼，アルミニウム精錬，石油化学，セメント，繊維などの基礎素材産業，および，金属工業，機械工業，化学工業などの重化学工業が，アメリカから最新技術およびオートメーション方式による大量生産技術が取り入れられたことにより，短期間に大きく発展します。

しかし，1973年，1979年の2度におよぶ石油危機のために，燃料費，原料費が高騰し，産業は停滞してしまいました。

そこで注目されたのが高度の加工技術を必要とする分野で，特に，エレクトロニクス技術を駆使した日本の製品群が，世界で圧倒的な強さを見せていきます。

しかし，1990年代に入ってから急速な円高となり，輸出をテコにして発展してきた日本の産業にストップがかかりました。日本製品の強さに対する欧米の反発もあって，これ以上，外国からの導入技術で技術革新をすることも難しくなってきました。

1994年以来，ゆるやかに景気の回復を見せ始めてはいますが，21世紀に向けて日本が取るべき根本的な課題は，日本独自の基礎研究の中から新しくリーディング産業を作りだすことと言われます。

eries, which Japan specialized in, cultivated fisheries may be the only way for Japan's fishing industry to survive.

• What are the prospects of Japan as an industrialized nation in the 21st century?

Japan's post-war industries are categorized into two types: the basic material industries such as steel, aluminum refinement, petrochemicals, cement, and fiber, and the heavy chemical industries such as metal, machinery, and chemicals. By introducing state-of-the-art technology and mass-production systems from the United States, these industries have developed rapidly in a short period of time.

However, due to the oil crises in 1973 and 1979, fuel and raw material expenses soared, which triggered a stagnation in industry.

Next, attention was turned to the electronics industry, which required a high-level processing technology. Japanese products demonstrated an overwhelming strength in the world market.

In the 1990's, when the yen rapidly appreciated, Japanese industries which had been propped up by exports, ceased to grow at the fast pace of the past. Also, American and European antipathy toward strong Japanese products affected the situation, making technological innovation using imported technology more difficult.

Since 1994, however, Japan has been gradually recovering from the economic recession. It is said that the task facing the country into the 21st century is to create its own leading industry from among fields in which basic research is now being done.

Q: 日本の物価は世界に比べて，まだ高いと言われているのですか?

日本の物価の高さは世界最高で，経済企画庁の1993年の調査によれば，東京の生計費はニューヨークの1.41倍，ロンドンの1.45倍，パリの1.36倍になっています。

たとえばハンバーガーの値段は東京で平均217円なのが，ニューヨークでは100円，ロンドンでは140円といった具合です。

しかし，1990年代半ばに入り，円高による輸入品の価格の下落，景気低迷による商品価格の低下，輸入規制緩和による「価格破壊」などの理由により，消費者物価の上昇率は1%を割り，衣料，家具，通信費などは逆に下がりはじめました。

Q: 日本の労働組合はどんな組織になっていますか?

A May Day scene

日本では企業別組合が，労働組合の基本的な単位となっています。つまり，ある企業の従業員になったら，その企業別組合の組合員になる，という形です。

各会社の組合は，同種産業の企業が集まって作った一種の企業別組合の支配下に入っています。そして，その企業別組合が集まって作ったのが，現在の「日本労働組合総連合会」です。労働組合員の約60%を組織しています。

他に，連合は労使協調路線だと批判して，共産党系の「全国労働組合総連合」(通称「全労連」)と，旧社会党左派系の「全国労働組合連絡協議会」(通称「全労協」)が組織されています。組織率は2つ合わせても9%ぐらいです。

• Are prices in Japan more expensive than in other countries in the world?

Prices in Japan are among the highest in the world. A 1993 survey by the Economic Planning Agency indicates that the living expenses in Tōkyō are 141% of those in New York, 145% of those in London, and 136% of those in Paris.

The average price of a hamburger, for example, is 217 yen, while it is 100 yen in New York and 140 yen in London.

However, the situation started to change in the mid 90's. The consumer price index fell below 1% as prices of items such as clothing, furniture and communication utilities began to go down. The reasons behind this change include the impact of the strong yen on prices of imported goods, the devaluation of merchandise due to the lingering economic recession, and price wars fueled by deregulation on imports.

• How are Japanese labor unions organized?

Most unions in Japan are company unions. In other words, when you are employed by a particular company, you become a member of that company's union.

Each company union is under the control of a type of industrial union composed of businesses in the same industry. In turn, industrial unions are part of the Japan Federation of Labor Unions, which organizes approximately 60% of unionized labor.

Other labor organizations include the Communist-run National Federation of Labor Unions, which accuses the Japan Federation of being too ready to compromise with business, and the National Labor Union Liaison Committee, which is affiliated with the left wing of the Socialist Party. Altogether

日本では産業別組合が育っていませんが，IMF・JC（全日本金属産業労働組合協議会）だけは，IMF（国際金属労働者連合）という国際的な組織に属していて，活発な活動をしています。組合加入者の約20%を組織しています。

しかし，雇用者数約3500万人の中で，労働組合に組織されているのは，1994年の段階で約1200万人です。組織率は年々落ちており，働く人の組合離れは進む一方です。

Q: 今，日本はどんな公害に悩んでいますか？

日本の公害の多くは，狭い国土に過剰な人口を抱えて，工場地と住宅地とが接近していることから発生しています。

三重県の四日市（よっかいち）市で起こった喘息（ぜんそく）のような呼吸器疾患は，近隣の石油コンビナートの排煙によるものであることが証明されました。有名な水銀汚染による水俣（みなまた）病や，カドミウム汚染によるイタイイタイ病も，近接する工場からの廃水が原因でした。

公害の発生源が特定できるものは，1967年の「公害対策基本法」によって規制されていますが，特定の何が原因とは言えない公害にも私たちは悩まされています。

大気中に放出された窒素酸化物や炭水化物が強い太陽光線で化学変化して起こす「光化学スモッグ」，工場や家庭の排水中の窒素やリンなどによって，海水中のプランクトンなどが過剰な栄養を得て発生し，魚や貝など貴重な海の生命を奪う「赤潮」，大気中の酸性汚染物質

these two organizations represent about 9% of union members.

Japan does not have industrial unions as such, but one organization, the IMF-JC (National Metal Industries Labor Union Committee) is affiliated to and actively involved in the International Metalworkers Federation, a worldwide organization. About 20% of union members come under the jurisdiction of this committee.

Of the 35 million people employed in Japan, however, in 1994 only 12 million belonged to unions. Union membership is declining each year, with fewer and fewer workers wanting to be involved.

• What kind of pollution is Japan facing now?

Pollution in Japan has worsened because of the overpopulated small land, where industrial and residential districts are located next to each other.

It has been proven that the asthma-like respiratory diseases observed in Yokkaichi City, Mie Prefecture, were caused by smoke dispersed from the local petroleum industrial complex. Minamata disease in Kumamoto Prefecture, caused by mercury poisoning, and *Itaiitai* disease in Toyama Prefecture, caused by cadmium poisoning, were both caused by waste water from neighboring plants.

In 1967 the Environmental Pollution Prevention Act went into effect, which regulates pollution from sources that can be determined, but pollution of which the cause is not known or is obscure is a matter of grave concern.

For example, photochemical smog is air pollution generated by nitrogen oxide and carbohydrate in the air which go through a chemical change in strong sunlight. Plankton in the sea, when excessively provided with nitrogen and phosphorus contained in waste water from households and factories, is responsible for the unpredictable red tide, which kills precious

を含んだ「酸性雨」，高速道路沿いの住居に被害を与える「騒音」……などなど，狭い日本の中で，日本人は公害と同居していると言ってもいいでしょう。

日本の税金

Q: 日本人はどんな税金を収めていますか？

税の内容は，自分の所得に課せられる「直接税」と，消費あるいは支出に課せられる「間接税」とに分けられます。

直接税には，所得税，法人税，相続税，贈与税などが含まれます。所得には国税のほかに地方税も課せられます。

間接税は商品の価格に加えられる3%の一般消費税に代表されます。負担するのは消費者ですが，国に収めるのは業者です。

1994年度予算で，日本の税金の収入のうち，直接税は68.1%，間接税は31.9%です。他の国に比べて，日本とアメリカは直接税の比率が高く，イギリス・ドイツ・フランスなどでは，間接税が50%ぐらいを占めています。

現在の税制では，21世紀の高齢化社会の社会保障制度の維持は不可能と言われ，間接税である消費税が引き上げられていく可能性が高くなっています。

Q: 世界に比べて日本の税金は高いですか？

日本の国民所得に対する租税負担率は，1994年では，国税と地方税を併せて24.1%です。金額にすると，718,172円です（大蔵省「財政金融月報」504号）。1990年では負担率は

sea life such as fish and shellfish. Sulfur oxide in the air creates acid rain, noise pollution affects residents near freeways—the Japanese live side by side with many types of pollution in their small land.

Taxes in Japan

• What kind of taxes do the Japanese pay?

Taxes in Japan are classified into two categories: "direct taxes" imposed on one's income and "indirect taxes" imposed on one's consumption and outgo.

Direct taxes include income tax, corporation tax, inheritance tax, and donation tax. Besides national taxes, local taxes are imposed on one's income.

The 3% consumption tax is representative of indirect taxes which is levied on goods. Purchasers pay the tax to merchants and it is the merchants' responsibility to pay the collected tax to the State.

Direct taxes account for 68.1% of the 1994 tax revenues of Japan, whereas indirect taxes account for 31.9%. In comparison with other countries, the ratio of direct taxes is higher in Japan and the United States, and that of indirect taxes is more than 50% in the United Kingdom, Germany and France.

It is feared that maintaining the social security system for the aging society in the 21st century will be impossible without raising the consumption tax.

• Are taxes in Japan high by world standards?

The tax burden ratio to the national income of Japan in 1994 was 24.1% with the national taxes and local taxes combined. The amount was ¥718,172 (from *No. 504 Monthly Financial Report* of the Ministry of Finance). The tax burden

28.1%でしたから少しずつ下がっています。

世界でいちばん税金の負担率が高い国はイギリスです。40%を超えています。次に高いのがイタリア，そしてフランスでそれぞれ33%，35%の負担です。一般的に，ヨーロッパ諸国は日本よりも税金の負担が大きいのですが，これらの国では間接税が半分ぐらいを占めています。

日本では税金は高いという意識を持っている人が多くいますが，それは所得から取られる直接税率が高いからと言えます。

日本の警察と犯罪

Q: 日本の警察にもFBIのような組織はありますか？

日本の警察は地方自治体に属していて，全国的な捜査組織はありません。例えば，東京警視庁は基本的にそれが所属する自治体，つまり東京都だけで活動する権限が与えられています。警察官は各都道府県内で活動するように決められているのです。

従って，オウム真理教のサリン事件，弁護士一家殺害事件など，同一の犯罪者が日本全国で犯罪を犯した場合の捜査のためには，FBIのような組織がほしい，という声も出ました。

国家公安委員会に所属する組織として警察庁がありますが，実際の捜査などには関わりません。警察に関する予算の確保，国の公安に関する警察の運営，全国的な幹線道路の交通規制などが仕事です。全国規模で動くことができるのは，過激派などに対応する公安調査庁だけです。

ratio in 1990 was 28.1%, and it has shown a gradual decrease.

The United Kingdom is one of the countries with the highest tax burden ratio, which exceeds 40%. In Italy and France it is 33 and 35% respectively. European countries generally have higher tax burden ratios than Japan, but the majority of their taxes are indirect.

If one has the impression that Japanese taxes are very high, that is because the direct taxes, or visible taxes, from one's income are quite high.

Police System and Crimes in Japan——

• Does Japan's police have an organization like the FBI?

The Japanese police belong to local municipalities, and there is no police organization that conducts investigation nationwide. For example, *Keishichō*, or the Metropolitan Police Department, is given the authority to operate basically in the municipality they belong to, in this case, the City of Tōkyō. Police officers are also supposed to work within their municipalities.

Some suggest that Japan needs an organization like the FBI which has control of all the police headquarters, in cases where crimes are committed by the same person or groups crossing prefectural borders, such as incidents with which the Aum Shinrikyō religious sect was involved in.

Even the National Police Agency, which belongs to the National Public Safety Commission, is not involved with actual investigations. The agency's job is to obtain the budget for the police, manage operations for national public safety, administer traffic control of main roads throughout the country, etc. The only organization that can develop nationwide investigation as a single entity is the Public Security Investigation Agency, which has expertise to deal with extremists.

しかし，各県の警察の連携で，全国捜査の効果を十分に挙げているのが日本の警察のすごさです。

Q: 日本にはどんな犯罪が多いですか？

Police box

1994年の犯罪件数は178万4432件で，事件の発生は前年よりも少し減っています。検挙率は43%で，ひところ落ちていた率が上がってきています。検挙率も殺人，強盗，放火などの凶悪なものに関しては89.1%という高率です（警察白書，1994年）。犯罪の内容は次の通りです。

窃盗犯	87.3%
住居侵入，器物破損など	6.3%
詐欺，横領，賄賂など	3.6%
暴行，傷害など	2.0%
その他	0.8%

1990年代に入ってからの特徴としては拳銃による犯罪の増加です。拳銃は日本では所持を禁じられていますが，暴力団以外の一般市民の世界にも拳銃が流れ込んでおり，暴力団抗争以外の拳銃による殺人，拳銃強盗などが増えています。

日本の防衛

Q: 日本はこれまでどこの国と戦争をしていますか？

日本の歴史上，他国と戦ったのは，663年に日本軍が唐(とう)（今の中国）・新羅(しらぎ)（今の韓国）の連合軍と戦った白村江(はくすきのえ)の戦いが最初です。次は1274年と1281年，2度にわたって日本に攻めてきた蒙古(もうこ)（元）軍との文永(ぶんえい)・弘安(こうあん)の役です。

However, the strength of the Japanese police is that they are able to conduct nationwide investigations effectively as prefectural police headquarters, especially, in cooperation with each other.

• What kind of crimes are the most common in Japan?

The number of known cases of crimes in 1994 was 1,784,432, which was down a little from the previous year. The arrest rate was 43%, which improved after a drop. For felonies such as murder, arson and armed robbery, the arrest rate was as high as 89.1% (*White Paper of National Police Agency,* 1994). The crimes in 1994 are classified as follows:

thefts	87.3%
trespassing, property damage	6.3%
fraud, embezzlement, bribery	3.6%
violence, injury	2.0%
others	0.8%

What characterizes crimes in the 1990's is the increase of crimes using guns, although guns are illegal in Japan. There has been an increasing number of crime cases where guns are used by people other than gangsters, in murders and armed robberies.

The Defense System of Japan

• What countries has Japan gone to war with?

The first war with a foreign country that appears in history was the Battle of Hakusukinoe in 663, in which Japan fought the allied forces of China and Korea. The second war was the Battle of Bun'ei and Kōan with Mongols in 1274 and 1281.

その後，豊臣秀吉が1592年，1596年の2度，朝鮮半島征服をねらって進攻しますが，1598年，秀吉の死で撤退しています。

江戸時代は鎖国で，他国との接触を断っていますが，明治維新後，再び日本の朝鮮に対する侵略政策は顕著になります。これに反対して1894年，清国が朝鮮半島に出兵し，日本との間に日清戦争が起こりました。

戦争は翌年，日本の勝利に終わり，朝鮮独立，遼東（りょうとう）半島・台湾・澎湖（ほうこ）諸島の日本への割譲などが決まります。

The Russo-Japanese War

しかし，ロシア・ドイツ・フランス3国はこれに反対し，特にロシアは満州占領を強化して，着々と南下政策をとりましたので，1904年，ロシアとの戦争が始まります。

結果は，翌年，日本の勝利。日本は朝鮮半島における優越権，南樺太（みなみからふと）の分譲などという成果を得ています。

その後，中国における権益の拡大をはかった日本は，中国との全面戦争に入り，ついには1941年，アメリカ，イギリス，オランダなどの連合国軍と太平洋戦争に突入します。

1945年敗戦。

他国との戦いが，近代国家になってからの100年たらずの間に，一気に増えているのが特徴的です。

Q: 自衛隊って，軍隊ですか？

日本国憲法は，その第2章第9条で，戦争の放棄を宣言しています。しかしそれは，こちらから戦争をしかけて，武力で紛争を解決するようなことをしないことを言っているのであって，自

Toyotomi Hideyoshi, in 1592 and 1596, made an attempt to conquer the Korean Peninsula, but in 1598 his men had to withdraw because of their lord Hideyoshi's death.

During the Edo period, the government took the National Seclusion policy and broke off all relations with foreign countries. However, after the Meiji Restoration, Japan's ambitions to invade the Korean Peninsula rekindled, posing a great threat to China. In 1894, the Ching Dynasty of China dispatched troops to the Peninsula, which started the Sino-Japanese War.

Japan's victory the next year resulted in the independence of Korea and the cession of the Liaodong Peninsula, Taiwan and the P'eng-hu Islands to Japan.

However, Russia, Germany and France were strongly opposed to it, and Russia launched its strategy of going south by trying to occupy Manchuria. The Russo-Japanese War broke out in 1904.

Japan once again won the war the following year and increased its rights in the Korean Peninsula while obtaining the southern part of Sakhalin.

Attempting to expand its interests in China, Japan wound up in an all-out war against China, and started the Pacific War in 1941 against the allied forces including the United States, England, and the Netherlands.

Japan lost the war in 1945.

The number of wars greatly increased during a period of only 100 years after Japan became a modern country.

• Are the Self Defense Forces a military organization?

No. The Constitution of Japan declares permanent renouncement of war in Article 9 of the 2nd Chapter. The post-war interpretation of this article was that Japan would never start a war or resort to military force to solve an interna-

分たちの国を守る権利を放棄したわけではない……という論理が戦後の政治の中で大勢を占めました。

それが日本に自衛隊が存在することになった主な理由で，最初は1950年に，警察予備隊として誕生しました。1952年には保安隊と改称。そして1954年には自衛隊法が成立して，自衛隊に育ってしまったのです。

自衛隊は陸海空からなり，戦闘機もあり，戦車もあり，地対空ミサイルもありますが，実際は軍隊ではないのです！

Q: 自衛隊の「戦力」は世界の中でどれくらいですか？

The Self Defense Force

1993年に421億ドルであった日本の防衛予算について言えば，アメリカの2507億ドル，ロシア790億ドルに次いで，3位に登場です。続いて，フランス，そしてドイツ，イギリス，中国と続きます。（国際戦略研究所（イギリス）「ミリタリー・バランス1994–95」から）

しかしGNP（国内総生産）は非常に高いので，それに対する比率は，アメリカの4.7%，韓国の4.2%，北朝鮮の，なんと25.2%に比べて，日本は1.6%です。

tional dispute and that the country had not given up the right to defend itself.

This was the major reason why the Self Defense Forces were formed in 1950 as the National Police Reserve. It was reorganized as the National Safety Forces in 1952, and in 1954, it developed into the Self Defense Forces with the enforcement of the Self Defense Force Law.

Though the SDF, which consists of Ground, Maritime, and Air Self Defense Forces, which has fighter planes, tanks and surface-to-air missiles, it is not actually a military.

- **How large is the "war potential" of the Self Defense Forces, if compared with militaries in other countries?**

In terms of the defense budget, which was $42.1 billion in 1993, Japan ranks third after the United States ($250.7 billion) and Russia ($79 billion). France, Germany, the United Kingdom, and China follow. (From *Military Balance 1994–1995* by the International Institute of Strategic Studies, London.)

However, since the Gross National Product of Japan is extremely high, the ratio of the defense budget to the GNP is only 1.6% for Japan. It is 4.7% for the United States, 4.2% for South Korea, and 25.2% for North Korea.

4

日本の社会

日本の人口と家族

Q: 日本にはどれくらいの人が住んでいますか?

1994年10月1日段階の日本の人口は，正確に言いますと1億2503万3542人です。この数は，中国，インド，アメリカ，ロシア，インドネシア，ブラジルに次いで世界7位の数字です。

しかし，国土面積が小さい日本の人口密度は，1km²あたり330人。1km²あたり27人というアメリカなんかとくらべれば日本はどこに行っても人ばかり……という外国人の皆さんの感想はもっともです。

Q: 日本の人口は増えているんですか，それとも減っているんですか?

人口は，1993年10月から1994年10月の間に，約27万人増えています。しかし，人口の増加率は1973年の第2次ベビーブームを境に，次第に減っています。

4

JAPANESE WAY OF LIFE AND SOCIETY

Japan's Population and Families

• What is the population of Japan?

As of October 1st, 1994, Japan had a population of 125,033,542 which ranks seventh in the world after China, India, the United States, Russia Indonesia, and Brazil.

Being a small country, Japan has a high population density of 330 people per km^2. Compared with the United States, where population density stands at only 27 people per km^2, it may seem that there are too many people in Japan wherever one goes.

• Is Japan's population increasing or decreasing?

Between October 1993 and October 1994, Japan's population increased by 270,000. Its rate of growth, however, has gradually slowed down after the "second baby boom" in 1973.

厚生省の人口問題研究所の推計によれば，西暦2000年には1億2700万人に達し，それから以降は減少しはじめて，2025年には1億2600万人，2050年には1億1200万人になると推定されます。

1994年国連の人口動態統計によると，人口の自然増加率は1000人につき，日本は2.9人，イギリスは2.6人，フランスは3.1人，そして中国は15.0人，インドは20.3人です。

Q: 日本人の平均寿命はどれくらいですか？

厚生省が発表した1993年の簡易生命表によると，男性の平均寿命は76.25歳，女性は82.51歳になっています。

これは世界一の寿命だそうですが，約60年前の1935年の平均寿命は，男性は46.92歳，女性は49.63歳でした。男女ともに，60年の間に30歳も寿命が延びているのです。

世界の長寿の国は，スウェーデン，ノルウェー，アイスランドなど北欧に多いようです。日本がこの国々と肩を並べたのは，社会的，経済的に，成熟した証拠でもあります。

Q: 日本の家族構成は平均して何人ですか？

1994年の総務庁統計局「家計調査報告」によれば，日本の1世帯当たりの人員数は，平均して3.63人です。

1955年の調査では，1世帯平均，ほぼ5人でしたから，約40年の間に，急激に出生率は下がり，家庭の構成は，夫婦と子供を中心にした核家族になってきました。

少なくとも，夫婦2人が2人の子供を生んでいかないと，人口は減少していくわけですから，平

The Institute of Population Issues of the Ministry of Health and Welfare estimates that by the year 2000 it will drop to 127 million, and will decrease to 126 million in 2025, and 112 million in 2050.

The United Nation's 1994 statistics of movement of population show that the natural population increase is 2.9 per 1000 people in Japan, 2.6 in England, 3.1 in France, 15.0 in China, and 20.3 in India.

• What is the average life span of the Japanese?

According to a 1993 survey by the Ministry of Health and Welfare, the average life span of the Japanese was 76.25 years for males, and 82.51 years for females.

These latest figures represent the longest life expectancy in the world. Back in 1935, the average life span was 46.92 years for males and 49.63 years for females. It has increased by as many as 30 years for both men and women over the past 60 years.

Other countries in the world which boast of longevity are mostly in Nothern Europe such as Sweden, Norway, and Iceland. Japan joined these countries as it matured socially and economically.

• What is the average number of people per household?

According to the *1994 Household Survey Report* compiled by the Management and Coordination Agency, the average number of people per Japanese household is 3.63.

In 1955, the number was about 5. During the following four decades, the birth rate has plunged and the number of "nuclear families" composed of only a couple and their children has grown.

Estimates for the next century show that Japan's population, which up until now has increased owing to the longer

均寿命が上がることで増えつづけている日本の人口は，2000年に入ってからは減少していくことになります。

Q: 昔と現代とでは，日本の家族はどのように違いますか？

武家の家父長制の延長で，明治時代でも，長男が家の財産と戸主権を相続することが，民法で定められていました。

しかし，第2次世界大戦後，このような家制度は廃止されました。社会と産業構造の変化に伴い，比較的，家制度の慣習を残していた農村部から，人々はそのような制約の少ない都会へと流出していきました。そして，恋愛結婚が見合い結婚を上回り，従来の家族の中の縦関係の代わりに，次第に夫婦を中心とした「核家族」になってきました。

日本の都市人口ランキング（1993年）
Population Ranking of Cities, 1993

（単位：1,000人　Unit：1,000 persons）

順位	市		人口	順位	市		人口
1	東京23区	Tōkyō 23 wards	7,927	18	相模原	Sagamihara	545
2	横浜	Yokohama	3,251	19	鹿児島	Kagoshima	532
3	大阪	Ōsaka	2,496	20	船橋	Funabashi	529
4	名古屋	Nagoya	2,095	21	東大阪	Higashiōsaka	496
5	札幌	Sapporo	1,704	22	尼崎	Amagasaki	489
6	神戸	Kōbe	1,468	23	新潟	Niigata	478
7	京都	Kyōto	1,394	24	静岡	Shizuoka	471
8	福岡	Fukuoka	1,214	25	八王子	Hachiōji	470
9	川崎	Kawasaki	1,168	26	姫路	Himeji	459
10	広島	Hiroshima	1,072	27	松戸	Matsudo	454
11	北九州	Kitakyūshū	1,015	28	松山	Matsuyama	452
12	仙台	Sendai	920	29	川口	Kawaguchi	443
13	千葉	Chiba	834	30	長崎	Nagasaki	439
14	堺	Sakai	799	31	横須賀	Yokosuka	438
15	熊本	Kumamoto	625	32	市川	Ichikawa	434
16	岡山	Okayama	595	33	浦和	Urawa	431
17	浜松	Hamamatsu	548	34	金沢	Kanazawa	431
				35	宇都宮	Utsunomiya	428

（「人口動態表」自治省　Ministry of Home Affairs, *Vital Statistics*）

average life expectancy, will decrease because of the smaller number of children a woman gives birth to in her lifetime.

• What major changes have occurred in the family?

Because of the influences of feudal patriarchalism, the civil law in the Meiji period determined that the eldest son would inherit the fortune and the patriarchal rights of the family.

However, the system was abolished after World War II. As the structure of the society and industry changed, many people left the rural areas where the old system still remained, and went to urban areas where such restrictions were rare. The number of arranged marriages, as opposed to "love marriages," has declined and the couple has gradually become the center of each household, instead of the traditional vertical structure of the family.

年齢別・性別人口 Population by Age and Sex

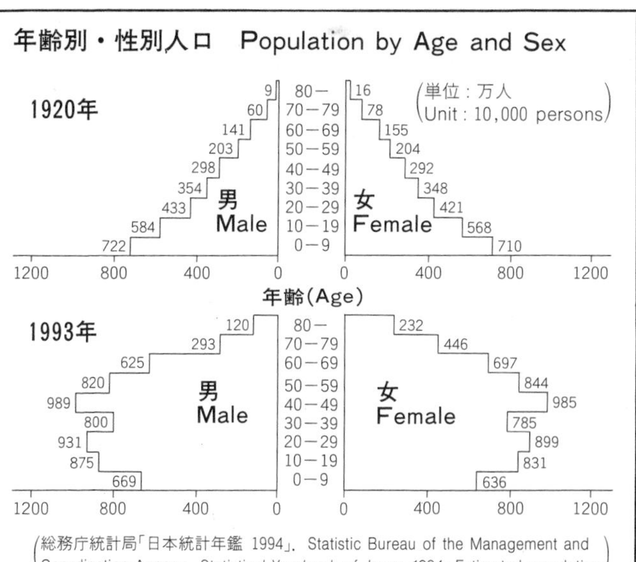

(総務庁統計局「日本統計年鑑 1994」. Statistic Bureau of the Management and Coordination Agency, *Statistical Yearbook of Japan 1994* : Estimated population)

日本人の特質

Q：日本人は集団で行動する，とよく言われるのはなぜですか？

社会の基本的な単位についての意識を，日本人は「家＝イエ」に置いています。ここで「イエ」というのは，「家族」の意味だけではなく，会社，学校，宗派など，運命を共にする「集団」も意味します。

封建的な家族制度や徒弟制度などはなくなりましたが，西洋の場合と違って日本の社会では「個」よりも「集団」が優先しています。終身雇用制度の会社がまだまだ多数を占めていますし，茶道や華道などの伝統的芸術には家元制度が残っています。

そのような集団の中では，集団への全面的な帰属が必要とされ，構成員はその集団に対する一体感をさえ抱くのです。その姿が外国人には，主体的な行動の欠如，個人的な責任感の希薄さ，と映るのだと思います。

しかし，集団が機能しなければ，構成員の存在もなくなってしまいます。「個」と「組織」のバランスを上手にとっているのが日本人，と言うこともできるでしょう。

Q：日本人は「本音（ほんね）」と「建て前（たてまえ）」を使い分けるというのは本当ですか？

日本人は自分の意見を言わない，2つの意見を使い分ける，と外国人からは批判を受けます。しかし，「個」よりも「集団」が優先されることによって秩序が保たれている日本の縦社会では，このほうが生き残りに必要だと考えられているのです。

The Characteristics of the Japanese

• What is the reason for the Japanese group behavior?

The basic unit of society in the Japanese mind lies in *ie*, which literally means "house" but implies other groups that bind people together, such as families, companies, schools and religious sects.

Although the feudal family system and apprenticeship no longer exist, emphasis tends to be placed on groups more than individuals, unlike in the West. Many companies have lifetime employment systems, and the hereditary system still remains in many traditional art forms such as tea ceremony and flower arrangement.

In such a society, a strong sense of belonging to groups is basically required, and in many cases their members identify themselves with the organization. To some foreigners, there might seem to be a lack of independent behavior and a sense of individual responsibility.

The Japanese, however, may argue that members cannot exist without the existence of groups. It can also be said that the Japanese maintain a good balance between organizations and individuals.

• Is it true that the Japanese differentiate between *honne* (true intention) and *tatemae* (enunciated principle) depending on the situation?

Some foreigners criticize the Japanese for not expressing their opinions and for having double standards. However, in the Japanese vertical society, where order is maintained by giving priority to groups rather than individuals, this is considered necessary for survival.

相手を傷つけることなく，効果的に物事を解決する方法としては，建て前が用いられ，自分の意見を強硬に通そうとすることは避けようとする傾向にあるのです。

Q: 日本人の精神に影響を与えている思想は何ですか？

Confucius

仏教と，儒教が，日本人の精神形成に大きな影響を与えています。

仏教は，人に生と死の観念を与え，念仏を通して，迷いや悩みを離れた悟りの境地に至ることを教えています。

儒教は，ご存知のとおり，孔子（こうし）（紀元前552－479）によって作られた思想体系で，宗教ではありません。その思想の中心には「仁（じん）」という言葉があります。「仁」とは人を愛することですが，キリスト教や仏教のような博愛の精神ではなく，親や兄弟を愛することです。まず「仁」によって家の中を治め，それを拡大して国家を治めようという考え方です。

日本の封建社会では，親や目上の人，ひいては国家元首を敬うという考え方は，支配者階級にとってはたいへん都合がいいものでした。このため近世では，武士が世襲的に支配していた封建社会を律する思想となり，明治時代になっても，儒教と西欧の近代的道徳とが結合した「教育勅語」が作られるなど，近代日本人の道徳形成にも重要な役割を演じ続けたのです。

Q: 日本人の性格にはどんな特質がありますか？

国際経営学者のロバート・マーチ氏は，「箱の中の日本人」という著書の中で，「日本ではグループ，会社，国家など，すべてが『箱』の中に入

The tactics of *tatemae* (enunciated principle) are often used in order to solve problems efficiently without hurting anyone, while pushing one's opinions too hard tends to be avoided.

• What ideas have an influence on the spirit of the Japanese?

Buddhism and Confucianism had a profound influence on the Japanese spirit and their world views.

Buddhism teaches concepts of life and death, and guides people, through chanting of the Buddhism invocation, to attain the state of emancipation (spiritual enlightenment) where there are no worries or hesitations.

Confucianism is the ideology of Confucius (552–479 B.C.) of China, and not a religion. One of the core concepts of Confucianism is *jin* (pronounced *ren* in Chinese), which basically means to love people, but this love is different from love or philanthropy taught in Christianity or Buddhism . It means to love one's parents and brothers and sisters first. Governing a house with *jin* and later expanding it to the level of the state is encouraged.

In the feudal era of Japan, the idea of respecting one's parents, elders, and the head of the state worked favorably for the ruling warrior class. The influence of Confucianism continued dominating the Japanese society into the Meiji period (1868–1912), when *Kyōiku Chokugo* (the Imperial Rescript on Education), incorporating the modern Western morality with Confucianism, was compiled, which played a crucial role in creating the moral values of the Japanese.

• What are some of the characteristics of the Japanese?

Business management professor Robert March, in his book titled *Reading the Japanese Mind*, explains an idea that is the key to understand the Japanese behavior. He points out that in

っていると考えると，日本人の行動様式が理解できる」と書いています。

つまり，せまい箱の中に入っているから―
・お互いに何を考えているのか分かるので，西洋人のように徹底的に討論しようとしない。
・箱の中で気持ちよく共存するために，自己主張をおさえ，習慣やしきたりを大切にする。
・統制がとりやすいので，効率がよく，上下関係がはっきりして，また，安全な社会が生まれる―というのです。

確かにこのように考えると「日本人はイエス・ノーがはっきりしない」「すぐ上司に相談する」などという外国人の非難の理由が分かるし，また経済大国になった理由や，犯罪の少ない安全な国である理由も分かりますね。

日本の教育

Q: 日本の現在の教育制度はいつできたのですか?

Terakoya

国民の誰もが教育を受けることができる近代的な教育制度が作られたのは，明治維新後の1872年です。江戸時代までは，庶民が教育を受けたのは寺小屋(てらこや)という施設でした。

当初，義務教育期間は4年で，身分・性別・貧富を問わないという建て前になってはいましたが，学業に必要な経費は学生が負担するのが原則でした。

また，次第に中央集権制のもとでの教育となり，1903年には教科書が国定となりました。1907

Japan, groups, companies, and the state are all contained in what he calls "boxes."

It is easy for the Japanese in a box to understand what others in the same box are thinking, so unlike Westerners, they do not bother to discuss matters to the end.

In order to live comfortably while getting along with each other within a box, the Japanese do not assert themselves too much and make the most of conventional customs and practices. He also mentions that in a "box" the whole system is easily controlled and thus efficient, and that there is a distinct hierarchy that makes a safe society.

This theory provides a good explanation for foreigners who criticize Japanese as being non-committal when they have to say either "yes" or "no," and always asking their bosses what to do. It also helps one figure out some of the reasons why Japan has become an economic giant, and why Japan is a safe country with a surprisingly low crime rate.

Education in Japan

- **When was the current educational system of Japan established?**

The original modern educational system was established in 1872. Before that, in the Edo period, *terakoya*—literal meaning "temple-shack"— was the place where ordinary people received an education.

At first the period of compulsory education was 4 years, and it was stated that everyone had an opportunity to study in the system regardless of one's social standing, sex, and whether one was rich or poor, as long as the students paid tuition and other necessary expenses.

The system developed under the centralized government, and nationally authorized textbooks came to be used in 1903.

年には義務制も6年になります。

そして，1945年の太平洋戦争の終結まで，国家主義の教育政策が強化されました。男女の教室も別にされていたのです。

1947年，新しく学校教育法が成立します。これによって現在の学校制度ができ上がりました。小学校6年，中学校3年が義務制となりました。その上が高校3年，大学4年となりますが，これは義務制ではありません。

Q:どういう学校がありますか？

次のような学校の種類があります。(　)内は基本的な就学期間です。

幼稚園(1–3年)
小学校(6–12歳までの6年間)
中学校(13–15歳までの3年間)
高等学校(3年間)
高等専門学校(5–5年6か月)
短期大学(2年間)
大学(4年間)
専修学校(1年以上)
専門学校(1年以上)
特殊教育学校

この中で小学校と中学校は義務教育です。高等専門学校は，工業，船舶に関する知識と技能の収得を目指したもので，中学を卒業すれば受験資格ができます。

専修学校は，料理，裁縫，簿記，建築設計など様々な技術を学習する学校です。中学校卒業者に対する高等課程，高校卒業以上の人に

Compulsory education was extended to 6 years in 1907.

Until the end of World War II in 1945, education policy based on nationalism was emphasized. At the time, male students and female students studied in different classrooms.

The new School Education Law was enacted in 1947, by which the current school system was formed. Under this system, 6 years of elementary school and 3 years of junior high school were made compulsory. Advanced education offered but not compulsory was 3 years of high school and 4 years of university.

• What are the schools like?

The following is a list of schools and age groups of students:

kindergarten (1 to 3 years)
elementary school (6 years between the age of 6 and 12)
junior high school (3 years between the age of 13 and 15)
high school (3 years)
technical college (5 years to 5 1/2 years)
junior college (2 years)
university (4 years)
special training school (more than 1 year)
vocational school (more than 1 year)
special education school

Elementary and junior high schools are compulsory. The technical college is designed to provide technical training for industrial purposes including shipbuilding for people with junior high school diplomas or higher academic education.

Special training schools teach skills such as cooking, sewing, bookkeeping and architecture design. It consists of the senior course for junior high school graduates and the profes-

対する専門課程に分かれています。

特殊教育学校は，身体が不自由な人のための学校です。

Q: 日本にはどれくらい学校がありますか?

公立，私立合計の数は下の通りです。

大学	552
短期大学	593
高等専門学校	62
高等学校	5,497
中学校	11,289
小学校	24,635
幼稚園	14,901
特殊教育学校	968
専修学校	3,437

(文部省「学校基本調査報告」1994年度)

義務教育である小学校，中学校の数は，戦後，急激に伸びた人口に追いつかず，1クラスの生徒数が50人を超えたこともありました。しかし，現在は40人以下に保たれています。

Q: 高校，大学への進学率はどれくらいですか?

1994年の数字では43.3%です(学校基本調査1994年)。1960年では10.3%ですから，35年の間に4倍以上の人が大学に行くようになっています。

高校への進学率もアメリカと同様に非常に高くなっており，100%近くですから，高校も義務

sional course for people with a high school diploma or higher academic education.

Special education schools provide education for people with physical disabilities.

• How many schools are there in Japan?

The total number of schools, both public and private, is as follows.

universities	552
junior colleges	593
technical colleges	62
high schools	5,497
junior high schools	11,289
elementary schools	24,635
kindergartens	14,901
special education schools	968
special training schools	3,437

(Ministry of Education, Culture and Science, *School Survey Report,* 1994)

Because of the rapid population growth after World War II, the number of students in a typical elementary and junior high school class once exceeded 50, but now it is kept under 40.

• What percentage of junior high school graduates go on to high schools, and what percentage of high school graduates go on to universities?

The percentage of high school graduates who go on to universities was 43.3% in 1994. The figure was 10.3% in 1960, which means four times as many students as 35 years ago enter universities.

Nearly 100% of junior high school graduates go on to high schools. Some say that high school also should be compulsory.

教育化すべきという声も出ているぐらいです。

高校卒業生の大学への進学率のトップはアメリカで，50%前後です。日本はそれに次いでいます。フランス，ドイツがこれに続き，さらにイギリスが続きます。

Q: 日本の学校と，アメリカの学校の違いはどこにありますか？

A successful candidate

アメリカでは医学部，法学部，商学部が大学院大学となっていることなど，大学の制度に違いがありますが，教育全体から見れば，現在の日本の学校の制度はアメリカと基本的には大きな違いはありません。

制度よりも，むしろ次のような違いを挙げなければならないでしょう。

例えば，アメリカには政府による「学習指導要領」などという画一的な教育方針の押しつけがないこと。公立の学校では，純粋な学問以外に実用的な技術の授業を選ぶことができること。

政府による教科書検定制度もないし，アメリカには過剰な受験戦争もありません。名高い

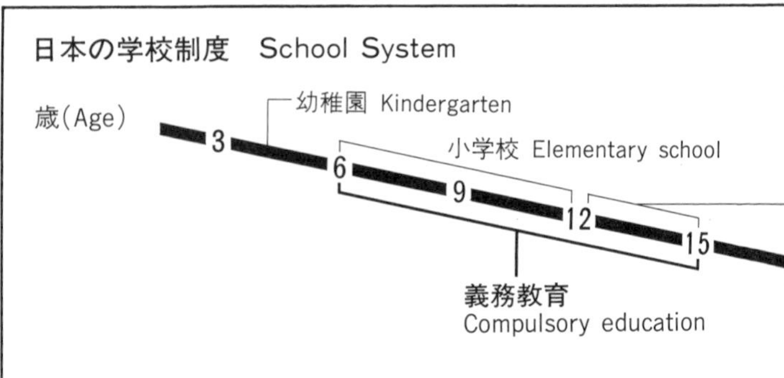

The percentage of American high school graduates going to universities is around 50%, which is the highest in the world. Japan ranks second followed by France, Germany, and the United Kingdom.

• What is the major difference between Japanese schools and American schools?

As a whole, the school systems of the two countries are not very different except that in the United States medical schools, law schools, and business schools are designed as graduate schools of universities.

Differences lie in other areas of the educational systems.

For example, American schools, unlike their Japanese counterparts, do not have a uniform "study guidance" system proposed by the government, and besides solely academic courses, they offer classes to acquire practical skills.

Neither textbook inspection systems by the government nor keen competition to enter colleges exist in the United

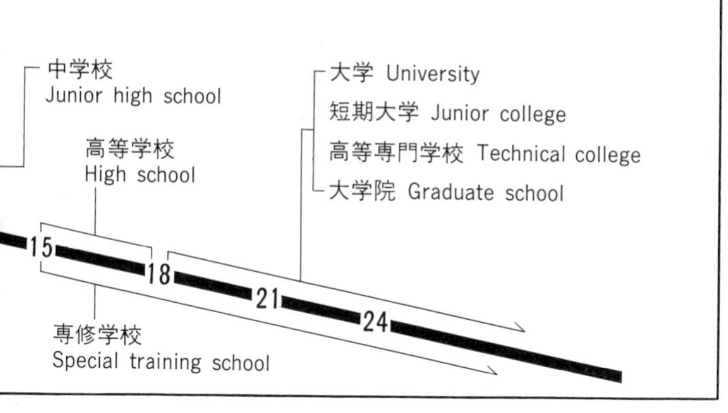

「受験地獄」にもかかわらず，日本では大学に入りさえすれば，後は遊んでいても卒業することができるとさえ言われます。

Q:どうして予備校や学習塾が多いのですか？

College entrance examination

おそらく日本ほど正規の学校以外に，学習塾がこれほど氾濫している国は，ほかにはないでしょう。イギリス，フランスなどでも受験や上級校への進学資格の獲得試験は難しいようですが，塾や予備校，ましてや有名な私立幼稚園に入るためのようなものはありません。

日本の親の中には，有名な幼稚園，というのは有名大学までそのまま進学できるという意味ですが，そんな幼稚園に子供を入れたがる人もいます。

在学中の小学生から大学入試に再挑戦しようとする人まで，多くの生徒が入試に首尾よく合格しようと塾へでかけるのです。

理由ははっきりしています。学校の授業を聞いているだけでは，入学試験の問題を解くことができないのです。ある程度の訓練をしないと，受験戦争に勝ち残ることができないのです。

これもすべて，いい会社に就職するため，また早く昇進するためには，有名な大学を出ていなければならないという「学歴社会」が原因です。

States. In spite of the infamous "examination hell," most Japanese universities are said to be hard to enter but quite easy to graduate from.

- **Why are there so many preparatory schools and cram schools?**

Japan is probably the country with the largest number of preparatory schools in the world. Although in some countries including France and the United Kingdom, entrance or qualifying examinations for advanced schools are very hard, no other countries have *juku*, or cram schools, even for entering prestigious private kindergartens.

Some Japanese parents are eager to send their children to such kindergartens affiliated with universities, which in most cases guarantee that the students can go on all the way to the universities, which are also considered prestigious.

Many students, ranging from elementary school pupils to those who make a second try to enter colleges, go to *juku* to prepare themselves to successfully pass entrance examinations.

The reason is clear. Just attending regular schools is not enough to survive in the examination war in terms of the knowledge necessary to be successful.

A society with a heavy emphasis on one's academic career, in which graduating from first-rate universities is among the first requirements to get quickly promoted, is behind all this obsession.

日本人と仕事

Q: 日本の会社とアメリカの会社の違いはどこにありますか？

基本的に次のような違いがあります。

1) 日本では基本的に終身雇用であることに対して，アメリカでは年次契約であること。

2) 昇進は，日本では基本的には年功序列であることに対して，アメリカでは実力主義であること。

3) 労働組合は，日本ではユニオンショップであるのに対して，アメリカでは産業別組合，職業別組合であること。

経済成長にブレーキがかかっている日本では，終身雇用を続けていては生き残ることができないと考えている企業も多く，給与や昇給を決める際に，従業員の能力・実績を査定する会社が増えつつあります。

Q: 働き者で有名な日本の労働者はどれくらい働いているのですか？

1991年の時点で，日本の労働者の年間労働時間は2080時間で，アメリカやイギリスの約1.1倍。フランスと比べると，なんと1.23倍でした。

しかし，1993年に改正された「労働基準法」により，日本の企業における最長労働時間は，「1日8時間；週40時間」に規制されることになりました。それに基づいて多くの会社が週5日制になってきています。

The Japanese at Work

• What are the differences between Japanese and American companies?

These are the basic differences:

1) In general, Japanese companies have a system of lifetime employment, while American companies employ workers on an annual contract basis.
2) Whereas in Japan employees are promoted according to length of service, in the United States promotion is mostly based on merit.
3) Japanese workers belong to company unions, while American workers belong to industrial unions.

The decline in the growth rate of the Japanese economy has caused many businesses to question whether they can survive while continuing to support a system of lifetime employment. An increasing number of companies are assessing the ability and work record of employees before they make decisions on salary and promotion.

• The Japanese are known for working long hours. Exactly how many hours do they spend at work?

In 1991, Japanese workers worked 2,080 hours per year, approximately 1.1 times as many hours as workers in Britain and the U.S., and 1.23 times as many hours as workers in France.

Under the revised Labor Standard Law of 1993, however, the maximum number of hours employees may work was limited to eight per day, and forty per week. Most companies are therefore moving toward a five-day workweek.

規模の小さい企業では，まだまだこの規制が守られていないのですが，日本の年間労働時間が，欧米なみになるのはそんなに遠い将来ではないでしょう。

Q: 休みはどれくらいありますか？

「労働白書」(1993年)によると，1991年の日本の年間休日数は 120日でした。これはフランスの 154日，旧西ドイツの 157日に比べると30日ほども違います。

ヨーロッパの人たちが1か月近いバカンスを楽しむという話は，今でも夢物語に近いものです。

1993年の労働基準法の改正で，休日に関しては，次のことが定められました。

・休日は少なくとも毎週1回

・年次有給休暇は，勤続6か月で，出勤率8割以上の者には10日

・勤続1年6か月以上の者には，勤続1年につき1日を，総日数20日まで加える

しかし問題は，日本の会社ではその休日をまとめて長期間とることができないことです。その権利があっても，長期の休暇届を出すと業績に支障を起こす心配がある，というのが実情なのです。

Q: 日本人はどれくらいの収入を得ていますか？

労働省の調査によれば，従業員30人以上の企業の，1994年の1人当たりの月間給与総額は40万1100円です。これには残業手当や特別給与(ボーナス)を月にならしたものも入っています。

金額的には，スイス，ルクセンブルクに次いで世界第3位という高額ですが，1時間当たり

This law is still often not upheld in small businesses, but even so it should not be long before the working hours of the Japanese are the same as those of workers in the West.

• What about holidays?

According to the *White Paper on Labor* (1993), in 1991 Japanese workers each had a total of 120 days off per year, around thirty days less than workers in France (154 days) and the former West Germany (157 days).

The month-long vacations enjoyed by Europeans still seems to be a long way off.

Under the revised Labor Standard Law of 1993, the following regulations concerning holidays were put into place:

——workers must have at least one day off per week.

——after six months at the same company, workers with an attendance rate of 80% or more are entitled to ten days paid leave.

——after eighteen months at the same company, paid holidays are increased by one day each year to a total of twenty.

The problem, however, is that in Japanese companies it is very difficult to take long holidays. Workers find it hard to take a lot of time off because they worry it will affect the operation of the business.

• What is the Japanese average income?

According to a 1994 survey conducted by the Ministry of Labor, the average monthly salary of people working for companies with more than 30 employees is 401,100 yen, which includes pay for overtime work and bonuses.

This figure is the third highest in the world next to Switzerland and Luxembourg. But in terms of wages per hour, Ameri-

の賃金で考えると，アメリカ人とドイツ人はもっと稼いでいます。日本と比べると，アメリカが140%，ドイツが146%になります。

日本人の購買力は，非常に物価が高いことを考えると，長時間働いて高い賃金をとっているわりに強くはないのです。

Q: 給料や地位はどうやって上がりますか？

Office workers

日本の企業の雇用形態は，終身雇用，年功序列が主ですから，いったん採用されると，賃金は学歴，勤続年数に応じて上がっていくのが普通です。

しかし，業務上の昇進は，実力によって個々に差異がありますから，年齢や勤続年数が同じでも，賃金には違いが生じます。

しかし，構造的な不況で，従来の年功序列型賃金制度では，企業は持ちこたえることができないと言われ始めています。

そこで，年功序列型の賃金制度の画一性を改めて，実力・成績にもとづく「年俸制」にする企業も，少しずつですが増えてきています。

年俸制をとっているのは，まだ，全企業のうち1%ぐらいですが，今後，日本でも年俸制が多くなってくることは間違いありません。

Q: 日本では単身赴任が多いのはなぜですか？

単身赴任と言われる転勤が多くなった理由として，次のことが挙げられます。

cans and Germans earn more than the Japanese—they make 140% and 146% respectively of what the Japanese do.

The purchasing power of Japanese, considering the outrageously high prices of things, is not as strong as it should be for the length of their working hours.

• How do employees in Japanese companies obtain promotions and pay increases?

Lifetime employment and promotion by length of service are the main features of the Japanese employment structure. Once someone has been employed, it is normal for their wages to rise in accordance with qualifications and length of service in the company.

However, because there are differences in the level of ability of employees, even among those of the same age or length of service, differences in wage levels do arise.

With the Japanese economy in a structural depression, the pressure is on companies to become more efficient, and some are unable to keep operating under the system whereby wages rise with length of service.

Consequently, a small but increasing number of companies are introducing an annual salary system based on performance to replace the uniformity of wage structures based on length of employment.

At present, only 1% of companies are using the annual salary system, but there is no doubt that the percentage will increase over time.

• Why do Japanese employees often leave their families behind when they transfer to other towns?

This type of transfer, known as *tanshinfunin*, has become increasingly common in recent times for the following reasons:

1つは，子供の教育のためです。受験戦争の激しい日本では，親の転勤につきあって，学校をかわることは，受験に不利になります。特に，子供が都会の進学校に通っている場合はそうです。

もう1つの理由は，交通の便の発達のおかげです。狭い日本ですから，これだけ空の便や新幹線が整備されますと，よほどの僻地でないかぎり，日本全国どこへ行くにもわずかの時間しかかかりません。週末に家族のもとに帰ってきて，月曜の朝早く赴任地に戻ることも可能になっているのです。

Q: 日本人は名刺がないと仕事ができないのですか？

日本ではビジネスに名刺はつきものです。初対面の人とは名刺交換するのが習慣として定着しているので，名刺を持たずに取引先を訪問することはありません。

日本人の名前は，音が同じでも文字が異なる場合がよくあります。正確な名前を相手に伝えるためにも必要になっています。

歴史的に見ると，古くは19世紀初期に使われていた和紙の名刺が残っていますが，これは氏名だけを手書きしたものでした。印刷した名刺は西洋から伝えられ，幕末開国のころ（1860年代）に外国人と接する役人が使ったのが始まりだったようです。

Q: ハンコは，いつ，どんなときに必要なのですか？

ハンコ（判子＝印鑑）には実印と認印の2種類があります。

Families must consider their children's education. In Japan, where competition in exams is fierce, changing schools may affect the child's chances of academic success. This is particularly the case when the child attends a school with a good academic reputation in one of the major cities.

Transport is another reason for the increase in *tanshinfunin*. Japan is a relatively small country, with a comprehensive network of air and rail links, and unless you are living somewhere very remote it takes only a short time to travel from one place to another. It is possible therefore to spend the weekend with your family and travel back to the workplace early on Monday morning.

• Can't the Japanese do business without business cards?

In Japan, business cards are indispensable for business. It's a well-established custom to exchange these cards with people you meet for the first time. The Japanese never visit clients without bringing business cards.

Japanese names are often pronounced the same, but are written differently. So these cards are further necessary to precisely convey people's names.

Historically *washi* calling cards, (some of which still exist) were used at the beginning of the nineteenth century, on which only the name of the person was hand-written. Printed calling cards were first introduced by the West. The card seems to have been initially used by Japanese officers who had to make contact with non-Japanese when the country opened its doors at the end of the Edo period.

• When and on what occasion are seals necessary?

There are two types of seals: registered seals and personal seals.

Personal seal

Registered seal

実印は，居住地の区市町村長に届け出をし印鑑登録をして，間違いなく本人の印鑑であることを証明できるようにしたものです。

まず一般の会社内では，自分の書いた書類に責任を持つという意味で押したり，他から回ってきた書類を承認したという意味で押したりします。会社員にとって，なくてはならないものです。

また，契約書などに同意する意志を示すとき，官公庁に届け出をするとき，指定された配達物を受け取るときなどにも使います。配達物などは，最近は署名でも済むことが多くなりました。

ふつう印鑑を使うときは認印でいいのですが，重要な取引上の文書，特に金銭取引の契約などには実印を使うことが求められます。

Q: 日本では転職する人は多いですか?

日本の会社の多くは，まだ，年功序列型で終身雇用です。ですから定年まで保障された会社から出ることは不安なことです。

転職しようとしても，「この人はなぜ前の会社をやめたのだろうか，なにか不都合なことがあったのでは……」などと，疑われることも心配なのです。

仮に転職ができたとしても，同じ賃金をもらうことができるかどうかも分かりません。日本のこれまでの労働環境では，転職していこうという人が少なくならざるをえないのです。

しかし，若い人たちの間では，会社に一生を捧げるという意識が薄れてきていることも事実で，また，年俸制なども導入されてくると，これ

Registered seals must be registered at the ward, city, or village mayor's office where the resident resides to identify that the seals actually belong to the person registered.

In most companies, businessmen stamp their seals on documents they've written to signify that they will be responsible for the contents, or to stamp documents circulated to signify officially that they have taken a look at them. Thus, seals are necessary in business interactions.

Also, seals are used to express agreement in contracts, to give notices to government offices, to receive designated deliveries, etc. These days, signatures are also acceptable in receiving deliveries.

For general use, personal seals are adequate, but registered seals are required for important business documents, particularly financial transaction contracts.

• Do many people switch companies?

Most companies still operate on a system of lifetime employment and promotion according to length of service, so people are generally unwilling to leave an organization which offers the security of guaranteed employment until they retire.

Even if people want to change companies, they worry that prospective employers will wonder why they left their previous job and assume they did so under unpleasant circumstances.

Even supposing that a person does succeed in obtaining a position in a different company, he or she is not assured of receiving the same salary. The employment structure in Japan, has until now made it difficult for many people to change jobs.

Among the younger generation, however, the idea of dedicating oneself to a particular company for life is losing popularity, and as the annual salary system becomes more

からは，自分の能力を生かすために転職に挑む人たちが多くなっていくと考えられます。

Q: 日本の会社の定年は何歳ですか？

1985年の段階で，60歳定年の制度をとる企業が，すでに50%を超えていました。それに拍車をかけるために，1986年,「60歳定年制法」が施行されました。

従って，現在，多くの企業が 60 歳定年に移行しています。厚生年金の給付も 60 歳からですし，これで日本にも「揺り籠から墓場まで」を保障する近代的な福祉国家の基盤が整ったと言えるでしょう。

問題は一歩進んで，60歳を過ぎた後も働きたいと願っている人の希望を実現させる方策ということになってきました。

Q: 働く女性と男性の割合はどれくらいですか？

Women Self Defense officers

1993年，企業に雇用された労働者の数は，男女あわせて5287万人です。そして，そのうち38%の2009万人が女性です。

女性が携わっている仕事は，サービス業，卸売り・小売業，金融保険業，事務などが主ですが，サービス業では約3分の2は女性です。

職場での男女の均等な機会と待遇の確保のために，1986年に「男女雇用機会均等法」が施行されました。これによって，職場への女性の進出も活発になり，男女の賃金格差も是正されてくるだろうと言われました。しかし，1992年からの不況のために，特に大学卒業の女性の就職難の時代が始まりました。

widespread, it is expected that more people will change jobs to make the most of their abilities.

• What is the retirement age in Japanese companies?

In 1985, sixty was the retirement age in over half of the companies, and to accelerate this trend the government introduced the Retirement-at-sixty Law in 1986.

Most companies therefore have moved to a system of retirement at sixty. This is the age at which pensions begin to be paid out, and with the introduction of this system Japan can be said to have established the basis of a social welfare state which looks after its citizens "from the cradle to the grave."

The problem has in fact progressed to one of how to satisfy those who want to continue working after sixty.

• What proportion of the workforce is female?

In 1993, the total number of people employed by businesses was 52,870,000. Of that number, 20,090,000 or 38% were women.

Women work mostly in the service industries, wholesale and retail sales, at financial institutions and insurance companies. In the service industries they comprise two thirds of the employees.

The Equal Employment Opportunity Law was passed in 1986 to ensure that men and women received equal opportunities and working conditions. It was predicted that this law would increase female participation in the workforce and correct the imbalance between male and female wages. Unfortunately, since the Japanese economy took a nosedive in 1992, it has become increasingly difficult for women, particularly university graduates, to find employment.

一方，パートタイム労働は毎年増え続け，1993年には日本の全雇用者のうち32%を占めていますが，そのうち約70%が女性です。男女雇用機会均等法の趣旨はまだまだ生かされていないと言えます。

Q: 結婚しても働く女性は多いですか？

結婚したことを理由に，女性に退職を求めたという時代は，日本でももう遠い過去のことになりました。育児休暇などの制度も確立されていますし，結婚して子供が出来ても，仕事を続ける人は多くなりました。

実際に，1993年の女子雇用者約2009万人のうち，67.2%が既婚者です。

20年ほど前の1975年では，女子雇用者は，約1160万人でしたから，今や働く女性は2倍に増えたわけですが，当時でもそのうちの60%は既婚女性でした。

年金

Q: 日本人はどんな年金に入っていますか？

1986年の法改正で，日本の年金制度は大きく次のように分けられます。

- 国民年金
- 厚生年金
- 共済年金

国民年金は，20歳以上の男女に義務づけられている年金です。自営業，主婦，学生，厚生年金に加入していない企業の従業員などが入ります。無職の人，外国人にも適用されます。

Part-time employment, on the other hand, is increasing every year, and part-time employees constituted 32% of the workforce in 1993, 70% of whom were women. It would appear that the objectives of the Equal Employment Opportunity Law are still a long way from being fulfilled.

• Do many women work after they marry?

Even in Japan it has been many years since women were expected to quit their jobs upon marriage. A maternity leave system has been established, and the number of women continuing to work after having children has increased.

In actual fact, of the 20,090,000 working women in 1993, 67.2% were married .

Twenty years ago, in 1975, the number of women in employment was approximately 11,600,000, so the number of women working has virtually doubled in that time. Even back then though, 60% of those women were married.

Pensions and Insurances

• What kind of pensions are provided for the Japanese?

With the revision of the pension law in 1986, the Japanese pension system consists of the following plans:

- National Pension
- Welfare Annuity
- Mutual Benefit Annuity

National Pension is required for people at age 20 or older who are self-employed, housewives, students, or employees of non-member companies of the Welfare Annuity system. It also applies to unemployed people as well as foreigners.

厚生年金は，民間の企業に勤める人のための年金です。

狭義では，共済年金は，国家公務員，地方公務員として勤める人のための年金です。勤労者，20歳以上の人は以上のどれかに加入することが原則です。

1993年現在，6927万6000人が，退職後にそなえて年金を払っています。一方，年金をもらう人は，1992年で2751万8000人です。

Q: 年金はどれくらいもらえるのですか？

国民年金でもらう年金は「老齢基礎年金」といい，25年以上加入していれば，月額6万5000円（1994年改正）を支給されます。

厚生年金でもらうのは「老齢厚生年金」といい，35年以上の加入で，同じく1994年の計算で，平均して21万4300円です。

共済年金は，国家公務員，地方公務員，その他の共済組合などによって，それぞれ違いがありますが，厚生年金よりも支給月額が，1〜2割多いようです。

Q: 日本人は平均してどれくらい生命保険をかけていますか？

生命保険文化センターの1994年の資料によると，日本における国民1人当たりの生命保険の契約高は1622.9万円となっています。

実は，日本の保険契約高は世界に比べてかなり多いのです。世界のいくつかの国と比べてみましょう。いずれも1993年の数字です。

アメリカ	482.2 万円

The Welfare Annuity is a pension for people working for private enterprises.

In a narrow sense, the Mutual Benefit Annuity is designed for national public servants and local public servants. The working population and people 20 or older in Japan must join one of the above-stated pension plans.

In 1993, 69,276,000 people were paying premiums for their pensions after retirement, whereas the number of people receiving their pensions was 27,518,000 in 1992.

• How much can one receive as pension money?

If you have participated in the National Pension Plan for more than 25 years, you will recieve 65,000 yen per month as "basic old age pension" (the 1994 revision).

In the Welfare Annuity plan, an average recipient with more than 35 years of membership will get 214,300 yen per month, as "old age pension."

The Mutual Benefit Annuity encompasses different plans depending on what mutual benefit association one belongs to, for example for national public servants, local public servants, etc., but the recipients are likely to get 10 to 20% more than the monthly amount provided by the Welfare Auunity plan.

• How much, on the average, are the Japanese insured for in life insurance?

According to 1994 data compiled by the Japan Institute of Life Insurance, the average amount of life insurance the Japanese were insured for was 16,229,000 yen per person.

The figure is extremely high by world standards. The following is a comparison with other countries based on 1993 figures.

United States	¥4,822,000

オランダ	414.3 万円
フランス	350.5 万円
オーストラリア	246.8 万円
韓国	231.1 万円
イギリス	199.2 万円
ドイツ	187.7 万円

日本人が保険に金をかける理由は，一つには国民総生産の伸びによる財政の余裕と言えますが，一方，国民が国の社会保障制度に信頼を抱いておらず，自衛策を講じていると言えないこともありません。

日本の医療

Q: 日本の医療施設は充実していますか？

1993年10月現在，次のような数字になっています。

	施設数	人口10万当たり
病院	9,844	7.9
一般診療所	84,128	67.4
歯科診療所	55,906	44.8

（厚生省「医療施設調査・病院報告）

しかし，施設の数だけでは判断ができませんので，人口10万当たりの医師数で比べてみましょう。歯科医を除きます。

旧ソビエト	（1985年）	421人
フランス	（1986年）	316人
ドイツ	（1991年）	306人
スウェーデン	（1990年）	287人
アメリカ	（1992年）	236人

Netherlands	¥4,143,000
France	¥3,505,000
Australia	¥2,468,000
South Korea	¥2,311,000
United Kingdom	¥1,992,000
Germany	¥1,877,000

Two of the reasons why the Japanese put so much money in insurance are individual financial stability that enables people to afford the payments and the desire to protect themselves because they do not trust the national social security system.

Medicine in Japan

• Are Japanese medical institutions fully equipped?

The number of medical institutions in Japan as of October 1993 was as follows:

	number	number per 100,000 people
Hospitals	9,844	7.9
Clinics	84,128	67.4
Dental clinics	55,906	44.8

(Ministry of Health and Welfare, *Survey Report on Medical Institutions*)

Compare the number of medical doctors (excluding dentists) per 100,000 people in Japan to those in other countries.

Former Soviet Union (1985)	421
France (1986)	316
Germany (1991)	306
Sweden (1990)	287
United States (1992)	236

日本　　　　(1992年)　177人

経済大国日本の医者の人数は，必ずしも多いとは言えないようです。

Q: いちばん多い日本人の死亡原因は何ですか？

人口10万当たりの主要な死因別の死亡者数を見てみましょう。

	1980年	1993年
悪性新生物（ガン）	139.2人	190.3人
心臓疾患	106.3人	145.5人
脳血管疾患	139.7人	95.9人
肺炎・気管支炎	33.8人	70.6人
事故	25.1人	27.9人
老衰	27.7人	18.7人
自殺	17.7人	16.5人

(厚生省「人口動態月報」)

上の表で特徴的なことは，ガンによる死亡率がますます高くなっていることですが，同時に心臓疾患も肺炎・気管支炎による死亡も増えています。医学は進歩を続けているというのに，1993年の病気による死亡者は，1980年に比べて121.1%という数字になっているのです。

一方，老衰で亡くなる人は減少し，日本が高齢化していく姿を知ることができます。

Q: 健康保険はだれでも加入することができますか？

官庁，公共機関，民間の事業体に雇われている人とその家族は，勤務先で強制的に健康保険組合に加入することになっています。保険

Japan (1992)	177

Japan, a great economic power, does not seem to have enough medical doctors.

• What is the most common cause of death in Japan?

You can find the answer in the following report, which shows the number and cause of deaths per 100,000 people.

	1980	1993
cancer	139.2	190.3
heart diseases	106.3	145.5
cerebrovascular diseases	139.7	95.9
pneumonia & bronchitis	33.8	70.6
accidents	25.1	27.9
old age (natural causes)	27.7	18.7
suicide	17.7	16.5

(Minister of Health and Welfare, *Monthly Report of Population Movement*)

The above chart indicates that the mortality for cancer, at the same time heart diseases, pneumonia and bronchitis is also on the increase. Although medical advancements are being made, the number of deaths by disease in 1993 was 121.4% of that in 1980.

On the other hand, the number of people dying of old age or natural causes has decreased, which means Japan's society is aging.

• Can anyone participate in the health insurance programs?

Upon joining an organization, the employees and their families employed by government offices, the private sector and public organizations automatically join the program. The

料は基本的に，労働者側と使用者側がだいたい半分ずつ払い込みます。

一方，雇用者であるかどうかを問わず，誰でも入ることができるのが，全国の市町村が公営している国民健康保険と言われるものです。小規模の会社の雇用者，自営業者，仕事をしていない人，学生，外国人などが対象となっています。

1961年，健康保険組合に加入していない住民は，必ず国民保険に入るように強制されていて，これが日本の社会保障制度の基盤を作っています。

日本の宗教

Q: 日本人はどんな宗教を信じていますか？

こんな数字があります。日本の宗教法人の報告に基づいた信者数の数字です。

神道系	1億1838万人
仏教系	8903万人
キリスト教系	151万人
その他	1115万人

（文化庁編『宗教年鑑1994』）

この数字を合計すると，なんと2億2007万人になってしまいます。これは各宗教団体が，亡くなったり脱会したりした人を信者数から外さないで報告しているからです。

一人一人の日本人に「信じている宗教は？」と聞くと，キリスト教や新宗教の信者を除いて「ありません」と答える人が多いはずです。

ところが，「あなたの家の宗派は？」と聞くと，「浄土（じょうど）宗です」とか，「日蓮（にちれん）宗です」という返事が

employee and employer pay about 50% each of the insurance premium.

Anyone can join the National Health Insurance program operated by municipalities throughout nation. The insured includes employers of small companies, self-employed people, unemployed people, students, and foreigners.

Since 1961, people who are not members of the Health Insurance Union have been required to join this program, which is the base of Japan's social security system.

Religions in Japan

• What religions do the Japanese have?

The following is the number of believers or followers of religions based on reports of Japanese religious corporations.

Shintoism	118.38 million
Buddhism	89.03 million
Christianity	1.51 million
Others	11.15 million

(Agency for Cultural Affairs, *Religious Yearbook 1994*)

Strangely enough, these numbers, when added up, amount to 220.07 million, which is far greater than the Japanese population. It is partly because the religious corporations surveyed did not report the number of people who ceased to be followers.

When one asks the Japanese, "What's your religion?" many of them, excluding Christians and followers of new religions, would answer "I have no religion."

However, when asked "What is the religion of your family?" they might answer "Jōdo sect of Buddhism," or

返ってきます。つまり，それぞれの家が昔から先祖を祀（まつ）るところとして持っている寺が，その人の宗教となっているのです。信仰心とは別問題なのです。

Q: 神道の神はいつ生まれたのですか？

Ise Shrine

8世紀の初めに編集された「古事記」と「日本書紀」に，神々の誕生の物語や神々の系譜が，神話として描かれています。

その神話によれば，最初の3神，天之御中主神（アメノミナカヌシノカミ），高御産巣日神（タカミムスビノカミ），神産巣日神（カミムスビノカミ）がいたそうで，この神は姿形がありませんでした。その後，伊邪那岐命（イザナギノミコト），伊邪那美命（イザナミノミコト）という男女の神が登場し，この2神が産み落としたのが，日本の8つの島だというのです。これらの神々は日本民族の先祖の象徴として崇拝の対象となっているものです。

神道では，自然の事物の一つ一つに宿る精霊が崇拝の対象となりますので，「八百万（やおよろず）の神」と言われるほどたくさんの神がいます。

Q: 神道は日本の国教なのですか？

神道は，日本固有の宗教です。仏教，儒教，道教などの外来の教義の影響を受けながら宗教として形成されていきます。

そして，江戸時代には「古事記」「日本書紀」に記録された神のみを忠実に信仰しようという考えが現れます。この考えは神の子孫とされる天皇を崇拝する思想と結びつき，朝廷を支配していた江戸幕府を倒す運動に発展しました。

明治維新後，神道は国家の保護を受け，天

"Nichiren sect of Buddhism." That means, the religion that each family has had since ancient times for the purpose of worshiping their ancestors has stayed with the household. Often times it has little to do with one's religious faith.

• When were the gods of Shintoism born?

The *Kojiki* and the *Nihonshoki*, two chronicles written in the early 8th century, depicts the ancient myths and history of Japan.

According to the myth, there existed the first three gods, Amenominakanushi-no-kami, Takamimusubi-no-kami, and Kamimusubi-no-kami, who were all invisible. Later, a god couple, Izanagi-no-mikoto and Izanami-no-mikoto, produced the eight islands of Japan. These gods are objects of worship at shrines as symbols of ancestors.

All natural objects and phenomena are also worshiped and considered as having gods, so there are myriads of gods in Shintoism, as the phrase goes *yaoyorozu-no-kami* (8 million gods).

• Is Shintoism Japan's national religion?

Shintoism is the indigenous religion of Japan. Influenced by Buddhism, Confucianism and Taoism, Shintoism later became ideologized.

In the Edo period, there was a view that encouraged the ancient faith in gods described in the *Kojiki* and the *Nihonshoki*. This view, associated with the worship of the Emperor as descendent of the gods, developed into a movement to overthrow the Edo feudal government.

After the Meiji Restoration, Shintoism was protected by the

皇を神格化するなどして，国家神道となります。太平洋戦争後は政教分離となり，神道は多くの宗教の1つの存在となっています。

Q: 日本の仏教にはどんな宗派がありますか？

仏教は広くアジアで信仰されている宗教です。東南アジアでは「小乗(しょうじょう)仏教」と呼ばれ，出家をして寺にこもり，修行をして，自分の悟りを得ることを目的としています。

中国，韓国を経て538年に日本に伝わった仏教は「大乗(だいじょう)仏教」と呼ばれ，広く大衆が救われるという考えに基づいています。

現在，日本国内で活動している仏教の宗派には，禅の3派を含めて次の13があります。

華厳(けごん)宗，法相(ほっそう)宗，律(りつ)宗，天台(てんだい)宗，真言(しんごん)宗，浄土(じょうど)宗，浄土真(じょうどしん)宗，時(じ)宗，融通念仏(ゆうずうねんぶつ)宗，日蓮(にちれん)宗，臨済(りんざい)宗，曹洞(そうとう)宗，黄檗(おうばく)宗。

Q: 「南無阿弥陀仏(なむあみだぶつ)」「南無妙法蓮華経(なむみょうほうれんげきょう)」とはどんな意味ですか？

「南無」というのは「神・仏などすぐれたものに服従し，尊敬する」という意味です。ですから，「南無阿弥陀仏」は「阿弥陀仏を敬い，その教えに従います」という意味で，広く仏教の各宗派で唱えます。

一方，「南無妙法蓮華経」は「妙法蓮華経に従い，その教えを守ります」という意味になり，こちらは日蓮宗で唱えます。

Q: 禅とはどんなものですか？

仏教の派の1つである「禅」の目指すところは，「心から迷いを無くして，真理に到達するために

State and the Emperor became deified. However, after World War II, the practice of religion was separated from the State, and Shintoism became one of the many religions in Japan.

• What sects are there in Japanese Buddhism?

Buddhism is a religion widely believed in Asia. Hinayana Buddhism, which aims at attaining emancipation or self-enlightenment by becoming a priest and undergoing acetic practices in a temple, is the major religion in Southeast Asia.

Buddhism which reached Japan in 538 via China and Korea is Mahayana Buddhism, based on the idea that the general public is saved by faith in Buddha.

Currently the number of Buddhist sects operating in Japan is 13 including 3 Zen sects: Kegon sects, Hossō sect, Ritsu sect, Tendai sect, Shingon sect, Jōdo sect, Jōdo Shin sect, Ji sect, Yūzū Nembutsu sect, Nichiren sect, Rinzai sect, Sōtō sect, and the Ōbaku sect.

• What do "*namu amida butsu*" and "*namu myōhō renge kyō*" mean?

Namu means "to obey and worship a superior existence such as gods and the Buddha." Therefore, when one prays "*namu amida butsu*," one says "I worship Amida Buddha and follow his doctrine." This prayer is used in many sects of Buddhism.

On the other hand "*namu myōhō renge kyō*" means "I obey *myōhō renge kyō* (sutra), and observe its doctrine," which is used in the Nichiren sect.

• What is Zen?

The purpose of the Zen sect, one of the denominations of Buddhism, is to meditate in order to eliminate hesitation or

Zazen

瞑想をすること」です。そのために，座って無心の気持ちで修行することを「座禅」と言います。

禅は紀元前からインドにあったものですが，後に達磨大師を含めた僧によって広められました。達磨は9年間も座り続け修行をしたと伝えられています。12，13世紀に，日本の僧たちが中国で修行をして禅宗を日本に伝え，現在，臨済宗，曹洞宗，黄檗宗が続いています。

Q:どんな時に寺に行きますか？

日本では人が亡くなりますと，ほとんど仏式で葬儀が行われます。そして，亡くなった人の遺骨は寺の墓に納めます。そのためにどこかの寺の檀家という，寺を支えるメンバーになっているはずです。

寺は本来，その地域に根ざしたもので，欧米のキリスト教会のような存在と言っていいでしょう。キリスト教の日曜礼拝のように，寺でも定期的な説法会が行われていたのです。

しかし，今ではこういう説法会に来る若い人は少なく，葬式の時以外には，めったに寺に行くことはありません。京都や奈良への観光旅行で有名な寺を訪ねる人は，数限りないのですが……

Q:どんな時に神社に行きますか？

神社も，寺の檀家と同様に「氏子」というメンバーで支えられています。しかし，信仰で結ばれた関係というわけではなく，神社のある地域の連帯といった感じでつながっています。

私たちが神社に行くのは，まず，正月の初詣

delusion and awaken to the truth. One of the practices used to acquire serenity of mind is *zazen*, which means to sit in silent meditation.

Zen existed in India before A.D., and it was later spread by priests including Bodhidarma, who is believed to have continued meditating in a sitting posture for 9 years. After studying in China, Japanese priests introduced the Zen sect to Japan in the 12th and 13th centuries. The existing Zen sects in Japan are the Rinzai sect, Sōtō sect, and Ōbaku sect.

• On what occasions do people go to temples?

Most funerals in Japan are conducted in the Buddhist tradition and the dead are buried according to Buddhist rites. Remains of the dead after cremation are placed in a grave at a temple. Therefore, a family whose member is buried in a temple becomes a supporting member called *danka*.

Originally a temple was deeply rooted in the community, and it was like a church in Christianity in the sense that regular lecture meetings for believers were held.

But very few young people now go to such events. Most people seldom go to temples unless there are funerals. However, temples in Kyōto and Nara, two representative ancient cities, are always filled with tourists.

• On what occasions do people go to *Shintō* shrines?

As temples have *danka* as their supporters, shrines have *ujiko*, which are not necessarily united by faith, but by a sense of community solidarity.

Most Japanese go to shrines at the time of their first wor-

Meiji Shrine

でです。その年の無事と多幸(たこう)を祈ります。

結婚式は今でも神前が人気。神社に行かなくても，式場に設けられた神殿の前で，結婚を誓います。

子供が生まれてから30日前後になると，「宮参り」といって，必ず神社にお参りします。

11月には，子供の成長を祝う「七五三」があり，3歳と7歳の女の子，3歳と5歳の男の子を着飾らせて神社に連れていきます。

そして，日本人の生活の中で大事な位置をしめる祭りは，神社の大事な行事です。私たちは何かを祝う気持ちの中で，神社を位置づけているようです。

Q: 日本にはキリスト教徒はどれくらいいるんですか？

文化庁編「宗教年鑑」によりますと，1992年のキリスト教の各派の信徒の合計は約151 万人です。

キリスト教は1549年から，フランシスコ・ザビエルをはじめとするスペイン，ポルトガルのローマ・カトリック教，イエズス会の宣教師によって，日本に広められていきました。そして，わずかの期間に信徒を獲得し，1580年には，その数は12万になっています。

しかし1640年，キリスト教は禁制となり，以後，1868年に明治維新で禁が解かれるまで，キリスト教徒たちは「隠れキリシタン」として生きていかざるを得なくなります。

太平洋戦争後の民主主義の時代になったとき，キリスト教の各派が日本に入り信者が急増

ship of the year on New Year's Day. They pray for happiness, peace and good health for the year.

For wedding ceremonies, Shintoism is among the first choices for couples. Many hotels and wedding ceremonial halls have Shintō alters, so couples do not have to go to a shrine to make a marriage vow.

When a couple has a baby, the baby is brought to a shrine around 30 days after his or her birth.

In November, on the occasion for celebrating *shichi-go-san* for girls at the ages of 3 and 7, and boys at 3 and 5, well-dressed children are taken to a shrine.

Festivals, which play an important role in the lives of the Japanese as popular annual events, are also conducted at shrines. The Japanese consider shrines as places of celebration.

• How many Christians are there in Japan?

According to the *Yearbook of Religions* compiled by the Agency for Cultural Affairs, the total number of Christians of various sects in Japan was approximately 1.51 million in 1992.

Christianity was first introduced to Japan in 1549, and was propagated mainly by Spanish and Portuguese Catholic missionaries of the Society of Jesus including Francisco Xavier. In a short period of time Christianity acquired many believers, and their numbers reached 120,000 in 1580.

After 1640, when Christianity was banned, persecuted Christians had no choice but to live as *kakure kirishitan* (hidden Christians) until the Meiji Restoration lifted the ban in 1868.

After World War II, when democracy and related ways of thinking were first introduced, the number of Christians

しましたが，最近の信者数の伸びは少ないようです。

Q: 新宗教にはどんなものがありますか？

数多くの新宗教がありますが，今も活動を続けているいくつかを，誕生の時代を追って挙げてみましょう。

江戸幕府末期から明治時代にかけて
- 神道系＝天理(てんり)教，黒住(くろずみ)教，金光(こんこう)教など

明治の末期から太平洋戦争終結まで
- 神道系＝大本(おおもと)教，生長(せいちょう)の家，世界救世教，PL教団など
- 仏教系＝霊友会(れいゆうかい)，真如苑(しんにょえん)など

戦後から1970年ごろまで
- 神道系＝天照皇大神宮(てんしょうこうたいじんぐう)教など
- 仏教系＝立正佼成会(りっしょうこうせいかい)，創価学会(そうかがっかい)など

1970年以降
- 神道系＝世界真光(まひかり)文明教団
- 仏教系＝阿含(あごん)宗，オウム真理教など
- その他＝幸福の科学など

信者の総数は，各教団の発表によれば，日本の全人口の1割に達すると言われています。

increased rapidly, but the speed of growth has slowed down in the past couple of decades.

• What kind of new religions exist in Japan?

Countless religions have existed. Listed below are some of the existing religions in chronological order of their establishment.

From the end of the Edo era to the Meiji era

- Shintoism—Tenrikyō, Kurozumikyō, Konkōkyō, etc.

From the end of the Meiji era to the end of the World War II

- Shintoism—Ōmotokyō, Seichō-no Ie, Sekai Kyūseikyō, Perfect Liberty Kyōdan, etc.
- Buddhism—Reiyūkai, Shinnyoen, etc.

From 1945 to 1970

- Shintoism—Tenshōkōtaijingūkyō, etc.
- Buddhism—Risshō Kōseikai, Sōka Gakkai, etc.

After 1970

- Shintoism—Sekai Mahikari Bunmei Kyōdan, etc.
- Buddhism—Agonshū, Aum Shinrikyō, etc.
- Others—Kōfuku-no Kagaku, etc.

The total number of such new religious believers is said to be about 10% of the Japanese population.

5

日本の文化

現代の文化

Q: 日本でノーベル賞をもらった人はどんな人ですか?

日本人で初めてノーベル賞を受賞したのは湯川秀樹でした。1949年に「中間子理論の研究」で物理学賞を受賞し，敗戦でうちひしがれていた日本人に明るい希望を与えました。

続いて1965年には朝永(ともなが)振一郎が，1973年には江崎玲於奈(れおな)が物理学賞を受賞し，1981年には福井謙一が化学賞を，1987年には利根川進が医学生理学賞を受賞して，科学技術の優秀さを世界に示しました。

Ōe Kenzaburō receiving the Nobel Prize

科学技術以外では，1974年に，元首相の佐藤栄作が平和賞を受けています。

文学賞は，1968年に川端康成が受賞しています。「雪国」「伊豆の踊り子」などの作者です。

5

CULTURE

Comtemporary Culture

• Who are Japan's Nobel laureates?

Japan's first Nobel laureate was Yukawa Hideki. He received a Nobel Prize in physics for his *Chūkanshi riron no kenkyū* (Study of Meson Theory) in 1949, giving hope to the Japanese people crushed by their defeat in the war.

Yukawa was followed by Tomonaga Shin'ichirō in 1965 and Esaki Reona in 1973, who were awarded Nobel Prizes in physics, and Fukui Ken'ichi, who was awarded a Nobel Prize in chemistry in 1981, Tonegawa Susumu, who was awarded a Nobel Prize in physiology and medicine in 1987, thus demonstrating to the rest of the world Japan's excellence in science and technology.

Outside the fields of science and technology, former Prime Minster Satō Eisaku received the Nobel Peace Prize in 1974.

In literature, Kawabata Yasunari received the Nobel Prize in 1968; he was the author of such works as *Snow Country* and *The Izu Dancer*.

そしていちばん最近では1994年に文学賞を受賞した大江健三郎です。「ヒロシマ・ノート」「万延元年のフットボール」などの作品があります。

Q: 日本にはどれくらい新聞がありますか？

Japanese daily newspapers

日刊新聞が何点発行されていて，1,000人当たりどれくらいの部数発行されているのか，主要な国を比較してみましょう。

	紙数	1,000人当たり
日本（1993年）	122	581部
アメリカ（1992年）	1,586	240部
ドイツ（1992年）	355	331部
イギリス（1992年）	101	383部
フランス（1992年）	77	205部
ロシア（1992年）	339	?

（ユネスコ「文化統計年鑑」1994年）

日本の新聞発行の特徴は，巨大な部数を持つ全国紙と，各地域の新聞とが共存していることです。しかも多くの新聞が朝刊と夕刊をセットにし，しかも各家庭への配達制になっていることも他の国にない特徴です。

また，都市の駅売りを中心に，多くのスポーツ新聞と，タブロイド版の夕刊紙が人気があります。

Q: いちばん売れている新聞はどれですか？

日刊新聞の朝刊の発行部数だけで比べると次のようになります。「日本新聞年鑑」（1994/95年）によると，読売新聞がいちばん部数が多くて，992.3万部，続いて朝日新聞828.3万部，毎日新聞400.8万部です。

The most recent Nobel laureate is Ōe Kenzaburō, who received the Nobel Prize in literature in 1994. Among his works are *Hiroshima Note* and *The Silent Cry*.

• How many newspapers are published in Japan?

The following is the number of daily newspapers being published and circulation per 1,000 people in Japan and other countries.

	No. of papers	per 1,000 people
Japan (1993)	122	581
United States (1992)	1,586	240
Germany (1992)	355	331
United Kingdom (1992)	101	383
France (1992)	77	205
Russia (1992)	339	?

(UNESCO, *Statistical Yearbook*, 1994)

The characteristic of Japanese newspaper publication is that nationwide, newspapers and local newspapers coexist in each region, and also most newspapers are delivered directly to homes and offices—a morning paper and evening paper as a set.

Sports newspapers and evening tabloid newspapers are quite popular and are mainly sold at kiosks of train and subway stations in urban areas.

• Which newspaper has the largest circulation?

When we compare the circulation of morning daily papers, *Yomiuri Shimbun* has the largest circulation with 9.923 million, followed by *Asahi Shimbun* (8.283 million) and *Mainichi Shimbun* (4.008 million) according to the *Japan Newspaper Yearbook* 1994/95.

これを世界の新聞と比べてみましょう。

ロサンゼルス・タイムズ	109.0万部
ニューヨーク・タイムズ	114.1万部
ウォール・ストリート・ジャーナル	181.9万部
デーリー・ミラー	263.0万部
ル・モンド	38.2万部
ウェルト	143.6万部
人民日報	400.0万部

(「日本新聞年鑑」1994/95年)

外国の新聞は朝刊専門紙か夕刊専門紙ですし,数字の多い少ないで新聞の人気を決めることもできませんが,各家庭への配達制度に支えられた日本の新聞の販売数字は,世界から見ると驚異的です。

Q: 日本にはどれくらいのテレビ局がありますか?

1993年の時点で,日本放送協会以外の民間放送会社の数は129社です。1953年のテレビ放送開始の時はわずかNHKのみ,しかも東京局だけでした。

現在次々と増えているのは放送衛星による衛星放送局,通信衛星によるケーブルテレビ局です。

Q: 日本ではどんなテレビ番組に人気が集まっていますか?

番組は,通例,3か月単位で変更されますから,視聴率の悪い番組は次々と消えていき,また新しい番組が誕生していきます。

1980年代まで人気があった歌謡番組は,1990年代に入ってからは少なくなりましたし,国

Let's compare these figures with those of other newspapers of the world.

Los Angeles Times	1.090 million
New York Times	1.141 million
Wall Street Journal	1.819 million
Daily Mirror	2.630 million
Le Monde	0.382 million
Die Welt	1.436 million
People's Daily	4.000 million

(*Japan Newspaper Yearbook,* 1994/95)

Unlike Japanese papers, most of the above papers are either morning papers or evening papers, and it is hard to measure the popularity of newspapers only by the circulation. But it is certain that the sales of Japanese newspapers, supported by their home delivery systems, are quite high compared to newspapers in other parts of the world.

• How many TV stations are there in Japan?

The number of private TV stations (excluding NHK) was 129 in 1993. When television broadcasting started in 1953, NHK, Nippon Hōsō Kyōkai, was the only station and Tōkyō was the only area where people could receive broadcasts.

There has been a rapid increase in the number of satellite broadcasting stations and cable TV stations using communications satellites.

• What kind of TV programs are popular in Japan?

The TV program lineup changes once every 3 months, and programs with lower audience ratings disappear as new programs are born one after another.

Programs featuring hit songs were popular until the 80's, but the number of such programs decreased in the 90's. Even

民的番組とまで言われた，NHKの紅白歌合戦の人気はかなり落ちて，中止がうわさされるなど，全体の番組の人気の傾向には大きな変化が見られます。

その変化の中で，人気を保っている番組のパターンを挙げておきましょう。

・スポーツ中継
・ニュースショー／ワイドショー
・クイズ番組
・連続ドラマ

Q: 日本人はどんな本や雑誌を読みますか？

日本人はいろんなタイプの本を貪欲に読みます。この日本人の読書好きな姿には次のような特徴があります。

1つは，週刊誌の人気があらゆる年齢の人に高いことです。政治・社会問題からヘアヌードやマンガ，連載小説などまで幅広く取り上げた，主に30代以上の男性向けのもの。次に芸能界の裏話や実用ページで売る女性週刊誌。いずれも売れ行きの上位を占めます。

Bookstore

そして，特に若い人たちに強い人気があるのがマンガ雑誌です。なかには毎週数百万部を売るものまであります。

多くのマンガは雑誌などに連載されて人気を得た後，単行本になってロングランで売れ続けています。

次に文庫本の人気です。価格が安く，また，通勤の混んだ電車の中でも読むことができる文庫は，今ではあらゆる分野の内容を網羅しており，日本人の読書には欠かせないスタイルの本となりました。

the legendary annual all-star music program by NHK broadcasted on New Year's Eve, the *Kōhaku Utagassen*, has lost much of its popularity. TV programming seems to be undergoing a major shift because of the changing needs of the viewers.

Under such circumstances, sports broadcasting, news shows, "wide shows" featuring news and gossip about celebrities, quiz shows, and serial dramas are maintaining their popularity.

• What type of books and magazines do Japanese read?

The Japanese are avid readers of various types of publications. Their reading trends are characterized as follows:

Weekly magazines are widely read by people of all ages. Magazines catering to men in their 30's, which deal with a wide range of topics such as politics and social problems, nude photos, comics and serial novels boast of large circulation. Ladies' weekly magazines featuring gossip and scandal involving celebrities, and articles providing practical knowledge of daily life also sell very well.

Magazines specializing in *manga*, Japanese-style sophisticated cartoons, are widely read by young people. Some of them sell several million copies every week.

Popular *manga* are turned into books after serializing in weekly magazines, most of which enjoy long-running popularity.

Pocket books, which are inexpensive and small enough to read in a crowded train, have become an integral part of the reading habits of the Japanese. Now virtually every genre of reading is available in this form of pocket book.

Q: 日本で有名なマンガ家はだれですか？

数え切れないほどたくさんの優れたマンガ家がいますが，絶対に挙げなければならない2人を紹介します

まず，手塚治虫（1928–1989）。

勇敢で心あたたかいロボット少年の活躍を描いた「鉄腕アトム」，ライオンの子が，森の指導者に育っていく姿を描いた「ジャングル大帝」など，数々の名作を描いています。日本のアニメーションの育ての親でもあります。

もう1人は長谷川町子（1920–1992）。3世代家族の日常の生活に繰り広げられる笑いを，嫁を中心に描いた4コマ・マンガの「サザエさん」は，1946年の新聞連載開始以来，日本全国の子供から大人までの心をなごませてくれました。今でも，本が売れ，テレビのアニメ・マンガの人気番組です。

Q: 日本のアニメーションの名作は何ですか？

Sailor Moon
© 武内直子　講談社　テレビ朝日　東映動画

日本は世界最大のアニメーション生産国です。anime という言葉が英語として定着しているほどです。古くは手塚治虫の「鉄腕アトム」のテレビ用アニメーションが，アメリカで「アストロボーイ」として人気を博しました。

最近では「セーラームーン」というテレビ・アニメがアメリカでも大人気になっています。そのほか数多くのテレビ用アニメが輸出され，世界中で見られています。

また現代のアニメ作家としては宮崎駿(はやお)が傑出していて，「風の谷のナウシカ」や「となりのトト

• Who are the famous comic book artists in Japan?

Although it is almost impossible to count the number of gifted comic book artists, two are definitely deserving of mention.

First of all, there is Tezuka Osamu (1928–89).

He produced a number of famous works, including *Astro Boy*, a story about the adventures of a brave and kind-hearted robot boy, and *Jungle King*, a story about a lion who is groomed to become the leader of the forest. He is also the father of Japanese animated film.

The other is Hasegawa Machiko (1920–1992). Her four-frame comic strip *Sazaesan* centers on a young wife, and gives a comic look into the daily life of her three-generation family. Ever since it first appeared in the newspaper as a serialized comic strip, it has warmed the hearts of adults and children throughout Japan. Even today, the comic strip sells well in book form, and the television animated program based on the strip is also very popular.

• What are some famous Japanese animated films?

Japan is the world's largest producer of animated films. The Japanese word *anime* has even gained currency in English. Older works include Tezuka Osamu's television animated film, *Tetsuwan Atomu*, which gained popularity in the U.S. as *Astro Boy*.

More recently, the television animated film *Sailor Moon* has also become very popular in the U.S. There are numerous other television animated films that have been exported abroad and are being watched around the world.

Another outstanding contemporary animated film artist is Miyazaki Hayao, whose works such as *Kaze no Tani no*

ロ」など，発表する作品すべてが大ヒットとなっています。

Q: 世界で活躍する日本の音楽家はだれですか？

Ozawa Seiji

戦後，多くの若い音楽家が，世界の音楽コンクールで入賞しており，世界を舞台に活躍しています。その最初の人がボストン交響楽団の常任指揮者の小沢征爾(せいじ)です。

バイオリンでは，まだ若いのですが，五嶋(ごとう)みどりがすでに一流の地位を築いています。演奏会で弦が切れても，コンサートマスターのバイオリンを借りて冷静に引き続けたというエピソードは，アメリカの教科書にも紹介されました。

ピアノではモーツァルトの演奏で世界的に有名になった内田光子がいます。

ソプラノでは中丸三千繪(みちえ)が，ヨーロッパで通用する歌唱力と舞台映えのする容姿を持っているといえるでしょう。

クラシック以外では，シンセサイザーを使った作曲，演奏をしている喜多郎と冨田勲，そしてアカデミー音楽賞を受賞した坂本龍一が世界的に活躍しています。

Q: 日本で人気のあるクラシック音楽は何ですか？

日本人の好みは世界とくらべてそんなに変わりませんが，日本で特別に人気のある2曲があります。1つはヴィヴァルディの「四季」で，とくにイ・ムジチ合奏団の演奏に人気があり，レコード・CDあわせて，日本国内で280万枚も売れています。

もう1つはベートーベンの第9交響曲「合唱付

Naushika (*Nausicaä of the Valley of the Wind*) and *Tonari no Totoro* (*My Neighbor Totoro*) have all become big hits.

• Which Japanese musicians are active internationally?

In the postwar period, many young musicians have won awards at international music competitions and are active worldwide. The first of these internationally acclaimed musicians is Ozawa Seiji, resident conductor of the Boston Philharmonic Orchestra.

Although she is still young, violinist Gotō Midori has already joined the top ranks of performers. An American textbook has even included an episode from one of Gotō's concerts, during which she borrowed the concert master's violin when one of her strings suddenly snapped, and coolly continued to play.

In piano, Uchida Mitsuko has become famous worldwide for her performances of Mozart.

Soprano Nakamaru Michie can be described as having singing talent as well as a striking stage presence winning respect in Europe.

Musicians outside of classical music who are active worldwide include Kitarō and Tomita Isao, both composers and performers of synthesizer music, and Sakamoto Ryūichi, who was awarded an Academy Award for Best Soundtrack.

• What kind of classical music is popular in Japan?

Although Japanese tastes are not so different from those of the rest of the world, there are two compositions that are especially popular among the Japanese. One is Vivaldi's *Four Seasons*, particularly the rendition by the I Musici Orchestra, which has sold 2,800,000 copies of records and CDs in Japan.

The other is Beethoven's Ninth Symphony with chorus. At

き」で年末になると，この曲のコンサートがほうぼうで行われ，この合唱に参加することを楽しみにしているアマチュア歌手たちが数多くいます。これは日本だけの異常現象ということができるでしょう。

Q: 今の若い日本人はどんな音楽が好きですか？

聴く，ということで言うならば，ロック，ヒップホップ，レゲエ，ユーロビート，ニューテクノなど，アメリカやイギリスのヒットチャートに入っているあらゆる音楽に，若者たちは興味を示しています。

しかし，自分たちで口ずさむことができるという点では，日本のオリジナルのポピュラー音楽の方が人気です。ユーミン(松任谷由実)，ミスター・チルドレン，その他，CDを出すたびに数十万枚を売る歌手やグループがいます。

日本では，カラオケが隅々まで普及していて，ヒットした日本のポピュラー曲はすぐにカラオケに取り入れられますから，これも人気を支える大きな力になっています。

Q: 世界に有名な日本の美術家はだれですか？

外国人の方々から見ると，たぶん，北斎(ほくさい)や歌麿(うたまろ)・写楽(しゃらく)という江戸時代の浮世絵師の名が出てくると思います。彼らの絵はゴッホやモネなど多くのヨーロッパの画家に影響を与えているのですから。

現在，世界的に人気のある日本画の画家としては，杉山寧(やすし)，東山魁夷(ひがしやまかいい)，高山辰雄，加山又造，平山郁夫などが挙げられますが，偶然にもみんな名前に『山』という字があるので「日本画の五山」といわれています。

the end of the year, concert performances of the Ninth are held everywhere, and many amateur singers look forward to singing in these choruses. This can probably be considered a phenomenon peculiar to Japan.

• What kind of music do today's young Japanese like?

For listening pleasure, young Japanese show interest in a variety of music on the hit charts in the U.S. and the U.K. such as rock, hip hop, reggae, Eurobeat, and new techno pop.

However, when it comes to singing songs themselves, domestic Japanese pop music is more popular. Yuming (Matsutōya Yumi), Mister Children, and other singers and groups sell several hundred thousand copies of each CD they release.

In Japan, *karaoke* has spread to every corner, and popular hit songs immediately are turned into *karaoke* music, which greatly helps to sustain the popularity of the songs.

• Which Japanese artists are famous worldwide?

Names that probably come to mind for many foreigners are Edo period *ukiyoe* printmakers such as Hokusai, Utamaro, and Sharaku. This may be because these artists have influenced many European artists such as Van Gogh and Monet.

Presently, internationally popular *nihonga* (Japanese-style painting) artists include Sugiyama Yasushi, Higashiyama Kaii, Takayama Tatsuo, Kayama Matazō, and Hirayama Ikuo; each of these five coincidentally have the character for mountain (*yama*) in their names, and so are known as "The Five Mountains of Japanese Painting" (*Nihonga no gozan*).

Q: 日本画は西洋の絵の手法とどう違いますか？

日本画という言葉は，明治以降，洋画，特に油絵が入ってきたことから言われるようになった言葉です。

一口に日本画といっても，実際は様々な流儀や様式があり，最近の日本画は洋画とほとんど変わらない画風の人もいます。

日本画の絵の具は岩絵の具を用い，にかわを媒材にし，紙や絹に描きます。

画材が異なるため，使う材料によって絵の具や墨のにじみを防ぐ方法，線の引き方，色彩のぼかし方などに伝統的な技法があり，かなりの修練が必要とされるという点が西洋の絵とは違います。

日本の伝統的な文化

Q: 短歌はなぜ日本人に愛されるのですか？

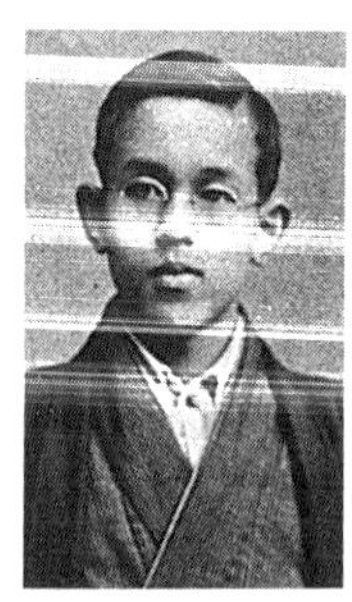

Ishikawa Takuboku

短歌は7世紀の初めには完成された，日本独自の詩の形式です。8世紀に編纂された「万葉集」にその原型があります。

5音，7音，5音，7音，7音の順に言葉をあてはめ，自分の感情や季節の情景を表します。俳句にある季語というものはありませんし，何を表現するかは自由です。

東海の　小島の磯の　白砂に
我泣きぬれて　蟹とたわむる

• How is *nihonga* (Japanese-style painting) different in technique from Western-style painting?

The word *nihonga* came to be used after the introduction of Western-style painting, especially oil paintings, after the Meiji period.

The word *nihonga* actually comprises a variety of schools and styles. The styles of some recent *nihonga* artists are similar to those of Western-style painters.

Nihonga uses mineral-based pigments with *nikawa* (hide or fishbone glue) as a medium on paper or silk.

There are traditional methods of blurring the colors, drawing lines, and preventing the blurring of ink or pigments that can vary with the type of materials used; these methods require extensive training and can be considered as aspects that differ from Western-style painting.

Traditional Culture of Japan

• Why do the Japanese love *tanka*?

The *tanka* is a uniquely Japanese poetic form perfected in the beginning of the seventh century. Its original form can be seen in the *Manyōshū*, an anthology of poems compiled in the eighth century.

Words which express the poet's feelings or the seasonal conditions are set into a 5–7–5–7–7 syllabic structure. With no "season words" as required in *haiku*, *tanka* allows more freedom of subject matter.

Tōkai no / kojima no iso no / shirasuna ni
(On the white sand of a rocky beach on a small island off the Tōkai coast)
Ware nakinurete / kani to tawamuru
(Soaked in tears, I play with a crab)

これは石川啄木(1886–1912)の歌です。声に出して読んでみますと，5・7・5・7・7という音のリズムが分かります。短歌の言葉の響きが，耳に快く響くことも，日本人に長く愛し続けられている理由の1つでもあります。

Q: 俳句はどうやって作られていますか？

俳句も日本独自の定型詩で，世界でいちばん短い詩です。17世紀末にこの形ができ上がったと言われ，江戸時代に盛んになり，芭蕉，蕪村という達人が現れます。

俳句は日本語の5音，7音，5音の3つの句に言葉をあてはめて作ります。例を挙げましょう。

古池や
蛙飛び込む
水の音

その語句の中に季節を表す言葉,「季語」と言われるものを必ず入れることが原則になっています。上の俳句では「蛙」が季節を表す言葉です。どんな語がどんな季節を表すかは，「歳時記」という本に書かれています。

Q: 歌舞伎はいつごろ始まったのですか？

1603年ごろに，出雲大社の巫女と称する阿国という女性が京都で演じた「念仏踊り」が初めであるとされています。

しかし，1629年に女性が出演することが禁止され，男性だけで演ずるようになり，元禄期(1688–1704)に現在の歌舞伎のスタイルができ上がりました。

明治になると西洋文化が急速に入ってきて，歌舞伎にもそういう新しさを取り入れようとした

This is a poem by Ishikawa Takuboku (1886–1912). If you read it aloud, you will hear the 5–7–5–7–7 rhythm. The pleasing resonance of its words is one of the reasons Japanese have long cherished the *tanka*.

• How are *haiku* composed?

Haiku is a poetic form unique to Japan and is the shortest poetic form in the world. It is said that the *haiku* form was created in the 17th century and flourished in the Edo period, when master poets such as Bashō and Buson emerged on the scene.

Haiku are composed of words accommodating a three-line, 5–7–5 Japanese syllabic structure. Here's an example.

Furuikeya	(An old pond)
kawazu tobikomu	(a frog jumps in)
mizu no oto	(sound of the water)

A basic rule holds that *haiku* must contain a *kigo*, or a word that expresses the season. In the above *haiku*, the frog is the seasonal word. *Saijiki* are compendiums of *kigo* which specify which words are associated with which season.

• When did *kabuki* originate?

Kabuki is supposed to have originated around 1603, when a woman attendant from the Izumo Shrine named Okuni performed a dance called *Nembutsu odori*.

However, in 1629, women were banned from the stage, leaving only men to perform; by the Genroku period (1688–1704), the current *kabuki* style was perfected.

With the Meiji period came a sudden influx of Western culture, and *kabuki* even attempted to incorporate some of

ことがあります。が，20世紀に入ってからは，古典劇としての伝統を守ることに方向が定まり，現在に至っています。

有名な歌舞伎役者の屋号(やごう)（俳優の名）は，血筋で伝えられていくという保守的な慣習に守られた世界です。

東京に歌舞伎座という常設の劇場があり，1年中，歌舞伎を演じています。

Q：能の始まりはいつごろですか？

Nō

能は，謡曲(ようきょく)と言われる歌と舞いで表現されます。奈良時代に大陸から入ってきた，軽業・奇術・歌舞などの雑多な芸能である「散楽(サンガク)」の中の歌舞が，日本の文化の中で独自の発展を遂げたもので，鎌倉時代の後半ごろには能の原型ができています。

1374年に将軍足利義満が，これを見て賞賛し，以後，彼の庇護(かご)を受けて発展します。そして，観阿弥(かんあみ)と世阿弥(ぜあみ)の父子が，芸術的な詩劇としての能と，その理論を確立しました。

現在，観世(かんぜ)，宝生(ほうしょう)，金春(こんぱる)，金剛(こんごう)，喜多(きた)の五つの流派があります。

Q：能と狂言はどんな関係ですか？

双生児の関係です。

能のルーツと同じ「散楽(サンガク)」から生まれたこっけいな物真似が，時代を経てこっけいな対話式の喜劇となっていったのが「狂言」です。

一方，真面目な，というとおかしいですが，謡いと舞いで表現する歌舞劇になったのが「能」です。

these new influences. However, in the 20th century, the trend focused on preserving *kabuki* as a traditional theatrical form, a trend which continues to this day.

It is a world that preserves conservative traditions, such as the practice of passing down the stage names of famous *kabuki* actors according to family lineage.

In Tōkyō, a permanent *kabuki* theater called the Kabuki-za stages performances throughout the year.

• When did *Nō* originate?

Nō theater is expressed through dance and music called *utai*. *Nō* is based on the song and dance taken from *sangaku*. *Sangaku* was a form of entertainment introduced from the continent during the Nara period and included acrobatics, magic, and song-and-dance. This song and dance developed in a uniquely Japanese way, and by the latter half of the Kamakura period, the stylistic features of the *Nō* theater were completed.

In 1374 the *Shōgun*, Ashikaga Yoshimitsu, watched a *Nō* performance and was deeply impressed; after this, the *Nō* theater advanced under his patronage. Kan'ami and his son Zeami developed the artistry of the *Nō* theatrical form, and established its theoretical underpinnings.

Today, there are five schools of *Nō* theater: the Kanze, Hōshō, Komparu, Kongō, and Kita.

• What is the relationship between *Nō* and *kyōgen*?

They are like twins.

A form of comic imitations originating from *sangaku*, also the origin of *Nō*, over the years developed into a farcical drama based on comic dialogue which then became *kyōgen*.

On the other hand, it was the more serious song-and-dance drama known as *utai* and *mai*, which became the *Nō* theater.

現在，能の上演をする時には，たいてい能，狂言，能という順序で行われています。

Q: 文楽(ぶんらく)の始まりはいつごろですか？

文楽は，人が後ろから人形を操る日本特有の人形芝居です。浄瑠璃(じょうるり)という音楽と語りに合わせて人形を動かします。1つの人形を3人が操ります。

このスタイルは安土桃山時代の終わり，文禄(ぶんろく)・慶長(けいちょう)(1592–1614)ごろにでき，江戸時代に入るとともに全国各地で興行されるようになりました。

その後，17世紀終わりごろ，竹本義太夫(ぎだゆう)によって人形を操る技術は高度になり，さらに物語もたくさん作られて完成の域に達していきます。

文楽は東京なら国立劇場，大阪では国立文楽劇場で定期的に公演が開かれています。

Q: 日本女性は皆，茶道，生け花の心得があるのですか？

いいえ。第2次世界大戦の終わりまでは，茶道も生け花も独身女性には欠かせないものでした。当時は「嫁に行く」ことが唯一の生きる手段であった女性にとって，これらは必須の教養課目だったのです。この傾向は第2次世界大戦前まで続きましたが，戦後，女性が社会に進出するにつれて少なくなり，現在は興味のある人だけがやっています。

それまでは，茶道や生け花に携わっていたのはすべて男性でしたが，生け花は，家の中の装飾に必要になるということで，茶道よりも早く江戸時代には，武家の女性のたしなみとなっ

Today, stagings of *Nō* usually present plays in the order of *Nō*, *kyōgen* and *Nō*.

• When did *bunraku* begin?

Bunraku is a form of puppet theater unique to Japan, in which the puppets are manipulated from behind. The puppets are manipulated in accordance with music and chants known as *jōruri*. One puppet requires the coordination of three people.

This form developed around the Bunroku and Keichō periods (1592–1614) at the end of the Azuchi-Momoyama period, and came to flourish in various regions beginning in the Edo period (1600–1868).

Around the end of the 17th century, Takemoto Gidayū perfected the manipulation of the puppets, while a great number of dramas were written which reached a new height of artistry.

Bunraku performances are regularly staged at the National Theater in Tōkyō and at the National Bunraku Theater in Ōsaka.

• Do all Japanese women know how to arrange flowers and perform at tea ceremonies?

No. Until the end of World War II both the tea ceremony and flower arrangement were prerequisites for marriage for single women. At that time, getting married was virtually the only option they had. However, as more and more women started playing an important role in the post-war society, this gradually changed, and currently both art forms are taken up by people who are truly interested in them.

A long time ago only men were engaged in performing tea ceremonies and arranging flowers. As an essential skill to decorate homes, flower arrangement was widely practiced among women in the warrior class in the Edo period (1600–1868).

ていました。茶道は，作法の修得や精神の修養に適しているということで，明治の中頃から，結婚前の女性の習い事として人気がでました。

Q: 茶道というのは，ふつうにお茶を飲むのとどう違うのですか？

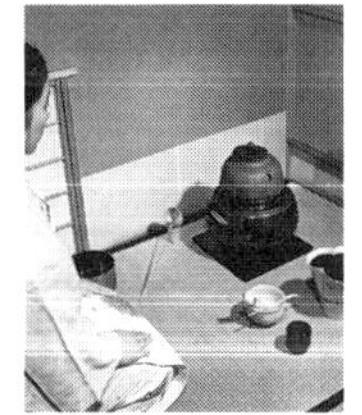
Tea making

茶道は室町時代の僧，村田珠光（じゅこう）(1422–1502)によって創造され，それを完成し，現代に続く茶道の形にしたのが千利休（せんのりきゅう）(1522–1591)です。

茶道では，抹茶という，茶の葉を粉末にしたものを用います。火をおこして湯を沸かし，抹茶をかき混ぜて飲むまでに，点前（てまえ）とよばれる様々な所作があり，これをいかに美しく行うかが第1のポイントです。

そして，第2のポイントは，茶会における主人（ホスト）と客（ゲスト）との心の交流です。主人は客をもてなすために，茶道具から掛け軸，花，花入れなどにいたるすべての取り合わせに気をつかいます。客も，その心配りを理解するためには洗練された教養と感覚を持っていなければなりません。

Q: 生け花とはどんなものですか？

形式化された生け花が始まったのは，室町時代からと言われています。それ以前には供花という，仏前に飾る生け花がありました。このため生け花には，神や仏の心を表すもの，あるいは宇宙の調和を表すものという観念があります。生け花の基本とは，いちばん上の花を「天」，下

The tea ceremony, which is considered to help one learn etiquette and develop mental strength, began gaining immense popularity in the middle of the Meiji period (1868–1912).

• How is the tea ceremony different from just drinking tea?

Tea ceremony was initiated by Murata Jukō (1422–1502), and perfected by Sen-no Rikyū (1522–1591), who exalted an everyday act of drinking tea to an integrated art form by stylizing manners of etiquette.

Maccha, or powdered tea leaves, is used in the tea ceremony. As one of the ceremony's most fundamental elements, the host is to follow various rules in every procedure of tea making, from making the fire, adding hot water to tea cups, stirring tea with a whisk until it gets foamy, to serving it.

Another important element is a shared sense of communication between the host and the guests throughout the ceremony. The host, in order to entertain his or her guests, takes utmost care in every step of the preparation processes, such as in choosing everything from tea utensils, to a hanging scroll, flowers, a vase and other amenities to go with the environment. The guests, in return, are expected to express their understanding of the host's consideration and gratitude toward the host's efforts.

• What is *ikebana*?

Ikebana, or Japanese traditional flower arrangement, was first stylized in the Muromachi period (1333–1568). Prior to that, people had a custom of offering arranged flowers to Buddha. The concept of *ikebana*, therefore, developed into one that expresses something Buddhistic or divine. It also embraces harmony with nature, symbolized by well-balanced

Flower arrangement

の花を「地」，中間を「人」とし，それらの調和を考えるというものです。

しかし，戦後になってからは，草月流のように，花以外の素材も使って現代感覚を盛り込み，造形芸術を目指す流派も生まれてきました。

現在，生け花には2000以上の流派があると言われています。池坊（いけのぼう）流，小原（おはら）流，草月流などが代表的な流派です。

Q: 家元制度というのは何ですか？

茶道，花道，香道，音曲などの伝統的な芸の世界で，その流儀の正統的な技法を伝え，その流派を統率する人を家元と言います。家元は世襲によって引き継がれていくのが普通です。

家元は大変な権力を持っています。茶道，華道などを教えるためには，家元が発行した免許状が必要で，その免許状を発行する権利は家元が握っているからです。

免許は段階的になっており，上の段階の免許をもらう度に免許料を納めなければなりません。いちばん上の段階になると，何百万円も支払うというケースもあります。

Q: どんな時に筆で字を書きますか？

学校では書道の時間がありますが，私たちが実生活で筆を使う機会はほとんどなくなりました。今では，公的な文書でさえ筆で書いたものは受け付けてくれないのです。筆を使うことがあるとすれば，次のような機会でしょう。あらたまったパーティーや何かの会合で，自分の名前

three basic sprays signifying *ten* (heaven / universe), *jin* (mankind) and *chi* (earth).

Since World War II, however, modern schools of *ikebana* such as the Sōgetsu school, which uses materials other than flowers, have appeared in an attempt to present this traditional flower arrangement as a kind of formative arts.

There are about 2,000 *ikebana* schools at present, including the Ikenobō school, Ohara school and Sōgetsu school.

• What is the *iemoto* system?

In the world of traditional Japanese arts such as tea ceremony, flower arrangement, incense ceremony, and traditional music, the *iemoto* is a person who consolidates his or her particular school by transmitting the correct methods of that school. The rank of *iemoto* is usually passed on by direct inheritance.

The *iemoto* has great authority. Licenses issued by the *iemoto* are necessary in order to teach such arts as the tea ceremony and flower arrangement since it is the *iemoto* who has the sole authority to grant these licenses.

Licenses are usually graded according to rank, and every time a higher rank is granted, a licensing fee must be paid. The highest ranks in some cases require a fee of several million yen.

• When do Japanese write with a brush?

Although calligraphy is taught in school, there are hardly any occasions in our lives today that require the use of the brush. Today, even for official purposes, writing with a brush is not accepted. Writing with a brush may be used for the following occasions: when writing your name at formal parties or meetings, when writing your name on special envelopes for

を書かなければならないとき，結婚や出産などのお祝いの祝儀袋や，お葬式の時の不祝儀袋に名前を書かねばならないときなどです。

しかし，それも筆でなければいけないわけではなく，サインペンなどを用いることが多くなりました。

Q: 盆栽はどうやって作りますか？

Bonsai

草木を小型の陶器などの容れ物に植えて，自分の好みの形に育てていく日本特有の園芸です。

育てる植物はいろいろですが，マツ，カエデ，ウメ，サツキなどが多いようです。

適切な土を用意し，肥料を与え，時には植え替えをして，幹や枝に針金を巻いて姿を整えたり，剪定（せんてい）をしたりします。

盆栽は1年，2年ではなかなかいい形には育ちません。何年も何十年もかけて育てていきます。

Q: 日本の陶磁器は有名なのですか？

Porcelain manufacture

奈良時代には中国から釉薬をかけて焼く方法が伝わりますが，この時代はまだ生活用具としての陶器でした。

平安時代には生活用の陶磁器の窯（かま）と，高級な用途のための2種類の窯が誕生します。そして室町時代に茶の湯が流行すると，高級で，また地方色が豊かな陶磁器が製作されるようになります。

江戸時代には上絵つけが始まり，焼き物の主流となり，有田焼や九谷焼などの磁器が作られ

monetary gifts given on celebratory occasions such as weddings or births, or on envelopes for condolence money given at funerals.

However, even these occasions do not necessarily require the use of a brush; more and more people now simply use a felt-tip pen.

• How are *bonsai* cultivated?

Bonsai is a horticultural art unique to Japan whereby grasses and trees are transplanted into small earthenware containers and are grown into desired shapes.

Although there are many different plant varieties, the pine, maple, plum, and azalea are particularly common.

Care for *bonsai* consists of selecting the appropriate type of soil, use of fertilizer, periodical repotting, wiring the branches or trunk to control the shape, and pruning.

A period of one or two years is not enough to allow *bonsai* to grow into the right shape. *Bonsai* takes many years, sometimes decades of nurturing.

• Are Japanese ceramics famous?

In the Nara period (710–794), the Chinese technique of glazing and firing was introduced to Japan, but only earthenware goods for daily use were made during this period.

The Heian period (794–1185) gave birth to two types of kilns; one appropriate for ceramics for daily use, and the other designed for various high-grade applications. In the Muromachi period (1333–1568), the popularity of the tea ceremony gave rise to the production of high-grade ceramics rich with regional variation.

The use of overglaze enamels began in the Edo period (1600–1868), and they became standard for ceramics of the

ました。特に有田焼には，オランダの東インド会社から大量の引き合いが来て，世界の陶芸家に影響を与えています。

Q: 日本の漆器はどこが優れていますか？

陶磁器は海外でチャイナと呼ばれていますが，ジャパンと呼ばれているのは日本の漆器です。

日本では縄文時代の前期の発掘物から，漆塗りの櫛やお盆が発見されています。日本書紀によれば，6世紀末に専門の漆器職人がいたことが書かれています。

漆器に用いるウルシは，世界各国で樹液の品質が違いますが，日本のウルシがもっとも品質がいいと言われています。

Q: 日本の刀は世界の刀とどう違いますか？

日本刀は西洋の剣と比べて柄が長く，刃は片刃で反りがあり，その重さから言っても，基本的には両手で持つように作られています。ちゃんばら映画で，片手で振り回しているシーンがありますが，実戦ではそうはいかない重さです。

軟鉄を心金に，鋼を皮金にして包む独特の鋳造法でつくられます。

刃の部分だけに焼き入れがなされるので刃に文様が現れ，鋼を鍛錬したことによる地肌の文様とともに固有の美しさが表れている，という

period, as with the Arita and Kutani porcelains that were being produced at the time. In particular, a great number of orders were received by the Dutch East India Company for Arita ware, and thus Arita ware came to exert influence on ceramic artists around the world.

• What is so prized about Japanese lacquerware?

Ceramics are known as "china" abroad, but "japan" is the term signifying Japanese lacquerware.

In Japan, lacquered combs and trays were found among unearthed goods from the early Jōmon period. According to the *Nihon shoki*, there were artisans specializing in lacquerware at the end of the 6th century.

The lacquer used for lacquerware differs around the world according to the quality of tree sap, and Japanese lacquer is considered to be the highest in quality.

• How are Japanese swords different from other swords from around the world?

Compared to Western swords, Japanese swords have longer hilts, are curved on one side of the blade, and the weight of the swords is designed for double-handed manipulation. Although in *samurai* films, one may see a scene in which the sword is manipulated by one hand, in actual fighting the heavy weight of the sword would not allow this.

Steel was welded into *kawagane*, or "skin steel," which was then welded onto the *shingane*, or "inner steel," made of more pliant steel—such were the unique forging techniques applied in swordmaking.

Since only the blade portion is tempered, it exhibits a temper pattern, which, along with the blade's patterned texture resulting from the forging process of the steel, are distinguish-

点に特徴があります。

Q: 人間国宝はどうやって決まるんですか?

伝統的な芸能の演技術や工芸の技術など，人や集団が技として受け継いでいるものを「無形文化財」と言います。

その中で特に重要な技を「重要無形文化財」といい，これを保持している人を，通称，人間国宝と称しています。これを指定するのは文部大臣です。

1994年現在，芸能関係，工芸技術関係それぞれ約40人の人間国宝がいます。人間国宝には年金250万円が与えられます。

ing features of Japanese swords.

• How are Living National Treasures designated?

Performing techniques for traditional forms of entertainment and techniques for traditional crafts that have been handed down by individuals or groups are considered to be "intangible assets."

Techniques considered particularly important are deemed "Important Intangible Assets," and persons who preserve these skills are commonly referred to as Living National Treasures. These designations are given by the Minister of Education, Culture and Science.

As of 1994, there are about 40 people designated as Living National Treasures representing various genres of traditional entertainments and crafts. Living National Treasures receive annual stipends of 2,500,000 yen.

6

日本人の衣食住

日本人の衣生活

Q: 日本人はいつから洋服を着るようになりましたか?

洋服が日本の実際の生活に取り入れられたのは明治になってからです。明治政府は軍装にヨーロッパの軍服を採用し，役人，郵便集配員や鉄道員にも洋服を着ることを定めました。近代国家の体制を早急に整えるために必要だと判断したのです。これによって，一般人の間にも，急速に洋服が普及しました。

しかし，女性の洋装は，一部の上層社会の婦人たちが，1883年に出来た社交場の鹿鳴館に着て現れただけで，大変高価ということもあり，次第に高まる国粋主義の風潮とともに，洋服は看護婦の制服だけになりました。

女性にも洋服が見られるようになったのは，女性がバスの車掌やタイピストなどの仕事に進出し始めた大正時代になってからのことです。

6

CLOTHING, CULINARY LIFE AND HOUSING IN JAPAN

Clothing of the Japanese

• When did the Japanese start wearing western clothes?

Western clothes were introduced in the Meiji period (1868–1912). The Meiji government adopted a European-style military uniform and decided that officials, mailmen and railroad workers wear western clothes because it felt that change was necessary for the Japanese government system to quickly transform itself into a modern state. This expedited the spread of western clothes among ordinary people.

However, dresses, partly because they were very expensive, were worn only by women in high society at parties held at the Rokumeikan, a western-style official party house built in 1883. As nationalism spread across the nation, western clothes were limited to nurse uniforms.

It was in the Taishō period (1912–1926) when working women such as bus conductors and typists started wearing western clothes in everyday life.

Q:どんな時に着物を着るんですか?

Young ladies in kimono at a Coming-of-Age ceremony

年配の人や，仕事の上で着物を着る必要がある人以外，ふだんに着物を着ている人はほとんどいなくなりました。

せいぜい正月に，年の初めの改まった気分を味わうために着物を着たり，年明けの仕事始めの日に，女性が着物で出勤する，といったところでしょうか。

お宮参りや七五三のお祝いには，子供に着せますが，最近はドレスやスーツを着せることも多いようです。

成人式，結婚式，卒業式や正式なパーティーなどの改まった席では女性が着物を着ることがあります。

日本舞踊など，日本の伝統の芸能を継いだり，学んだりする人や，料亭の仲居(なかい)さんなどは和服を着ることが必要になります。

木綿の浴衣(ゆかた)は着物の一種で，夏に着たり，和風の旅館に泊まると寝巻きとして出してくれますが，略式の着物ですから，公式の場には出られません。

日本人の食生活

Q:日本人の平均的な食事はどんなものですか?

日本人の食生活は西洋化が進んで大きく変わり，ずいぶんと多様になりました。いちばん大きい変化はパン食の取り入れです。朝食にはパンに簡単な卵料理，ミルク，そしてコーヒーや紅茶で食事をする人が多くなってきました。

サラリーマンの昼食は，昔は弁当を持ってい

• On what occasions do people wear *kimono*?

Very few people, except some elderly people and those who wear them out of professional necessity, wear *kimono* daily.

On New Year's Day some men and women wear *kimono* to bask in the holiday mood, and some women wear them to work on the first day of work every year.

Babies are often dressed in *kimono* on their first visit to a shrine, and at the *Shichi-go-san* Festival, many children are dressed in *kimono*, although a growing number of parents choose western clothes over *kimono* on this occasion.

The Coming-of-Age day, wedding ceremonies, graduation ceremonies and formal parties provide women opportunities to wear *kimono*.

People in the world of traditional arts such as Japanese dancers, and workers at Japanese-style restaurants need to wear them more often than most people.

Yukata, which is made of cotton, is a kind of *kimono* worn in summer or as pajamas offered at Japanese-style inns. Since it is considered very casual, one is not supposed to wear it on formal occasions.

Culinary Life of the Japanese

• What is the typical eating habit of the Japanese?

Japanese eating habits have become quite diverse, with a lot of changes it has gone through becaue of westernization. One of the major changes is the introduction of bread. Many people eat bread, eggs, milk, and drink coffee or tea for breakfast.

Decades ago, salaried workers took often packed lunches

School lunch

く人も多かったのですが，今では会社の近くの食堂で，洋風から和風まで……その日の好みで様々です。

多くの小・中学校では給食があります。栄養のバランスを考えた食事ですが，時には和風とも洋風ともいえない不可解なメニューもあります。

家に帰って食べる夕食もあれこれ取り混ぜたもので，和風，中華，洋風など様々です。御飯に汁物，そして肉，魚，野菜などのおかず，というのが日本の食事の平均的な内容です。一般的に言って子供たちは，昔からの和食よりもハンバーグなど洋風を好むので，家庭の夕食の傾向は子供たちに引っ張られています。

Q: 日本人は米を毎日食べますか？

Japanese food

朝食にパン食が増えたり，昼食は麺類で済ます人も多いということは事実ですが，1日に1回は米を食べないと気が済まないという人が多いことも事実です。

しかし，次の農林水産省「食糧需給表」の数字があります。日本人1人1日当たりの米穀類の供給量です。

	1960年	1980年	1993年
米	314.9g	216.3g	189.7g
小麦	70.6g	88.3g	88.2g

上の表から，米を食べる量がずいぶんと少なくなっています。ところが，小麦の量はほとんど同じです。

実は，日本人の食事は，米やパンなどの炭水化物よりも，肉や乳製品や果物にますます頼るようになってきているのです。

to work, but nowadays any kind of dishes ranging from Western food to Japanese food are available in restaurants near office buildings.

Most elementary and junior high schools have school-lunch programs, offering well-balanced meals in sometimes eclectic varieties.

Dinners served at home are also diverse, including dishes of Japanese, Chinese and Western cooking. A typical dinner consists of rice, soup, and several dishes containing meat, fish, and vegetables. Generally speaking, children prefer western food such as hamburgers to traditional Japanese dishes, and many households are inclined to cater to their tastes.

• Is rice still the mainstay of the Japanese diet? Do people eat it every day?

It is a fact that many Japanese feel like eating rice at least once a day, although some have bread for breakfast and noodles for lunch.

The following *Table of Food Supply and Demand* by the Ministry of Agriculture, Forestry and Fisheries indicates the amount of rice and flour consumed by one person per day.

	1960	1980	1993
Rice	314.9 grams	216.3 grams	189.7 grams
Flour	70.6 grams	88.3 grams	88.2 grams

The above chart shows that while the amount of rice consumption has greatly decreased, that of flour has stayed almost the same.

In fact, the diet of the Japanese has become increasingly dependent on other dishes such as meat, dairy products, and fruits rather than carbohydrates such as rice and bread.

調査によれば，1960年と1993年では，肉類は6倍，牛乳，乳製品は4倍，果実は2倍に増えているのです。

Q: 日本人がいちばん好きな食べ物は何ですか?

日本人の食生活は洋風，和風，中華風など多様になり，好みも多様になりましたので，何が一番人気かは明確ではありません。

ただ，大衆的なレストランの調査で，いちばん注文が多いのは，ハンバーグ，カレーライス，スパゲティだそうで，一般の家庭でもこの3種が多いようです。

外国の人から見ると，日本と言えば，寿司，てんぷら，すきやき……となるのでしょうが，そんなに毎日食べているわけではありません。

Q: 醤油(しょうゆ)はいつごろから日本で使われているのですか?

文献に「しょうゆ」という言葉が登場するのは室町時代の中期，16世紀の終わりごろです。室町時代の終わりごろには，醤油は急速に人々の間で使われるようになります。

しかし，すでに奈良時代以前から，醤油の原型と思われる醤(ひしお)というものがありました。この醤は，穀類や鳥や獣，魚肉，野菜，海藻などに塩を加えて発酵させたものです。醤油や味噌は，これから発展したものなのです。

すでに江戸時代に，現在も使われている溜(たまり)，濃口(こいくち)，薄口(うすくち)などの様々な醤油の種類が生まれています。

Q: 味噌はいつごろから日本で使われているのですか?

味噌は奈良時代にその前身があったようで

A survey reveals that in 1993, people ate six times as much meat, four times as much milk and dairy products, and twice as much fruits, as they did in 1960.

• What is the favorite food of the Japanese?

Because the Japanese eating habits have diversified, it is hard to choose only one dish as their favorite food.

According to a survey conducted by popular restaurants, the most frequently ordered items are hamburges, curry and rice, and spaghetti. These three dishes are favorites at home as well.

In the eyes of foreigners, *sushi*, *tempura* and *sukiyaki* may be typical Japanese dishes, but the Japanese do not eat them every day.

• How long has *shōyu* (soy sauce) been used in Japan?

The first known descriptions of *shōyu*, or soy sauce, appeared in literature during the middle of the Muromachi period (1333–1568) and at the end of the 16th century when soy sauce became common among ordinary people.

However, the original form of soy sauce dates back to the pre-Nara period (710–794), when *hishio*, fermented sauce containing grain, meat, fish, vegetables, sea weed and so forth was used. Soy sauce as well as soybean paste (*miso*) developed from this sauce.

Different kinds of soy sauce used presently, such as *tamari* (thick sauce), *koikuchi* (dark sauce) and *usukuchi* (lighter sauce) were made during the Edo period (1600–1868).

• How long has *miso* (soybean paste) been used in Japan?

The original form of *miso*, or soybean paste, is said to have

す。平安時代にはすでに味噌を売る店があったということです。

味噌は，蒸した大豆に麹と塩を混ぜて発酵させたものですが，鎌倉時代に寺院などでも作られており，15–16世紀の戦国時代には，兵士たちの食糧として重用されていました。

一般庶民に普及したのは，醤油と同じく室町時代からです。

Q: 豆腐が健康にいい，と言われるのはなぜですか？

豆腐には，大豆の植物性たんぱく質が豊富で，カルシウムやカリウムなどの無機質やビタミンBも含まれており，肉や牛乳からたんぱく質をとる場合に比べて脂肪が少なく，カロリーも抑えられるのです。

豆腐は中国で作られたのが最初で，奈良時代に日本に伝わっています。

味が淡白なので，刻んだ長葱や擦りおろしたショウガのような薬味を添え，醤油をかけてそのまま食べたりしますが，調理法は数百種もあると言われています。

Q: 正しい箸の持ち方は？

最近の若い人には正しい持ち方ができない人が大勢います。家庭の食事も洋風が多くなり，子供のころにフォークやスプーンなどに慣れてしまったからでしょう。

まず，2本を少し離して，平行に人指し指の根元と親指ではさみ，上のほうの1本の中ほどを，人指し指の先の腹，中指の先の背，そして親指の先の腹ではさみます。下のほうの1本は，

How to hold chopsticks

existed in the Nara period (710–794). In the Heian period (794–1185), there were already stores selling *miso.*

Miso is made from soybeans, which are steamed and mixed with salt and *kōji* (fermented rice, barley or beans). It was made at temples in the Kamakura period (1185–1333), and in the age of civil wars in the 15th and 16th centuries, it was used in rations for soldiers.

It was in the Muromachi period (1333–1568) when *miso* became popular, as *shōyu* did among the general public.

• Why is *tōfu* said to be a health food?

Tōfu, made from soybeans, is rich in vegetable protein, calcium, potassium and Vitamin B. It is considered healthful because it does not contain as much fat as meat or milk, and its calorie contents are very low for the amount of protein it provides.

Tōfu was made in China and it was introduced to Japan in the Nara period (710–794).

When eaten uncooked, since it is light in taste, it is often topped with spices such as finely chopped green onions and grated ginger, and soy sauce is poured over it. It is said that there are several hundred recipes using *tōfu.*

• What is the proper way to hold chopsticks?

Many youngsters nowadays are not able to hold chopsticks properly. Perhaps the reason is that they are more accustomed to eating westernized food with knife and fork.

To hold chopsticks properly, start with separating the two chopsticks, then placing them horizontally in parallel with each other on the index finger and under the thumb. Put the middle of the upper chopstick between the finger pad of the

中ほどを中指の先の腹と薬指の先の背ではさみます。てこのようにして動かすことができるのは上のほうの箸(はし)だけです。

箸でフォークのように食物を突き刺すこと，箸の先をなめること，箸の先を楊枝(ようじ)代わりに使うなどするのはマナー違反です。

Q: 日本は魚が豊富ですが，和食ではどんな料理法がありますか？

新鮮な魚なら薄く切った刺身がいちばん，という人が多いでしょう。ワサビと醤油をつけて食べます。

生の魚は握り寿司にして食べる方法もありますが，寿司の握り方はけっこう訓練を要しますので，自宅で作ることは比較的少ないようです。

いちばん手軽で多いのは塩焼きです。塩をちょっと振りかけて焼きます。マグロなどの赤身の魚を除き，どんな魚も塩焼きができます。

醤油をベースにしたタレをつけるのが，照り焼きです。醤油味か味噌味で煮ることもあります。このような料理法には，サバなど，油ののった魚が向いているようです。

てんぷらにするとおいしいのは，小エビ，クルマエビ，イカや白身の魚です。

ムニエルにするなど，洋風の料理法も取り入れられていますが，少なくとも魚に関しては，和食の伝統のほうが強いようです。

index finger and the nail side of the middle finger. Place the thumb on top of the upper chopstick. Use the finger pad of the middle finger and the nail side of the ring finger to hold the middle of the lower chopstick. Using the principle of leverage, you only move the upper chopstick to pick up food.

It is considered ill-mannered to poke food with chopsticks, to lick the tips of the chopsticks, or to use chopsticks as toothpicks.

• What type of cooking techniques are used to prepare fish commonly eaten in Japan?

If the fish is fresh enough, *sashimi*, or thinly sliced raw fish, is preferred by many people. It is eaten with soy sauce and Japanese horseradish.

Raw fish is also eaten in the form of *sushi*, but since preparing *sushi* requires special skills, it is not often made at home.

The most frequently used cooking technique is grilling with salt sprinkled on top of the fish. Any fish except for red-meat fish such as tuna can be cooked this way.

Teriyaki is prepared by marinating fillets of fish in a soy-sauce-based sauce, and grilling while basting the sauce. Sometimes fish is boiled over low heat using soy sauce or *miso*, soybean paste. Fish with a lot of fat such as mackerel is suited for these cooking techniques.

Shrimp, prawn, squid and white-meat fish are eaten as tempura, or deep-fried.

Western techniques such as meunière have been adopted in the Japanese culinary, but Japanese traditional cooking is still most common as far as fish is concerned.

Q: 日本酒はどうやって作りますか？

Sake

米と米麹と水を原料として，発酵させて，濾したものが「清酒」です。

まず米を精米して洗い，糠を取り除きます。適度な水を吸収させたあと，水をきり，蒸して麹と水を加え，約20日間をかけて発酵させます。

それを圧搾機にかけて酒と酒粕に分離します。分離した酒を静かに置いておくと，清酒と滓に分離します。

この清酒を濾過器で濾して，香りと味を調え，加熱して殺菌したものを6か月以上，20度以下で熟成します。その上でさらに調合・調整をして加熱殺菌してでき上がりです。

後は瓶に詰めて出荷されます。

日本人の住生活

Q: 日本の家の平均的な広さはどれくらいですか？

Apartment complexes

1993年の住宅統計調査によれば，日本の1住宅当たりの面積は，1戸建て住宅で約120m²です。共同住宅などを含めると，約89m²です。

1人当たりの床面積に換算すると約25m²だそうです。しかし，これをアメリカの61m²や，イギリスの35m²という数字と比べると大変低い数字で，日本の住宅がかつて「ウサギ小屋」と呼ばれたのももっともです。

しかし，これでも1960年代と比べれば2倍近くの面積になっていますが，これからは住宅を購入すること自体が難しくなっていますので，1人当たりの床面積の数字が増えることは期待できないようです。

• How is *sake* or Japanese rice wine made?

Seishu, which means pure *sake*, is made from rice, rice-fermented *kōji*, and water.

First, wash the rice to remove the rice bran. After letting the rice absorb water, drain it, steam it, mix it with *kōji* and water, and let it ferment for 20 days.

The ingredients are compressed by machine to separate them into *sake* and *sakekasu* (leavings). The *sake*, by letting it stand for a while, is separated into *seishu* and *ori* (dregs).

The *seishu* is filtered, and its flavor and taste are adjusted. Disinfected by heating, *seishu* is cured at a temperature lower than 20 degrees for more than 6 months. After that, final adjustments are made before it is re-disinfected by heating.

The *seishu* is then bottled and shipped.

Housing in Japan

• What is the average size of Japanese residences?

A 1993 residential survey shows that the average size of an independent house is about 120 m^2 and including condominiums and apartments, an average of 89 m^2 per household.

The average area for one person is 25 m^2, which is much smaller than 61 m^2 in the United States and 35 m^2 in the United Kingdom. This is the reason why Japanese houses were once called "rabbit hutches."

Yet the area of 25 m^2 is twice as large as it was in the 1960's. Since the housing situation in Japan is bleak for buyers, chances are slim that the area available for each person will greatly increase in the future.

Q: 日本では家の値段はどれくらいしますか？

東京では，都心に出るのに1時間ぐらいの所に，100m²ぐらいの土地付きの1戸建てを買おうとすると，5000万から6000万円はかかるのです。80年代後半から90年代初期のバブル経済の後，土地の値段は下がりましたが，それでも異常に高いものです。売り出される家自体が少なく，都会では，価格，供給の両面で，家を買うことが困難な状態が続いています。

1993年の全住宅数のうち，持ち家の比率は60%ですが，1983年より2%下がっています。これからもこの比率は下がっていくことは間違いありません。

Q: 東京の便利な所に部屋を借りると，いくらぐらいかかりますか。

部屋の広さや所在地で随分違いますが，例えば，通勤時間30−40分以内で，ワンルームか1DKの1人用の住まいの場合，1か月の家賃は6万円くらいからです。

ちょっと広くて駅から近いと，8万円くらいにはなるでしょう。日当たりなど，環境の良さを加えたら10万円を超します。

バスルームがない古いタイプのアパートなら，上記の半分くらいの家賃です。

日本では，入居の際に家賃の5か月か6か月分のお金を支払わなくてはなりません。通例，敷金と言われる保証金が家賃の2か月分，礼金と言われる契約金のようなものが1，2か月分，そして，不動産屋に1か月分くらいの仲介手数料を払います。

敷金はそこを出る時，部屋を元の状態に戻

• How much does a typical house cost in Japan?

If you were to buy a house in Tōkyō with a lot of 100 m^2 within one-hour commuting radius, you would have to pay 50 to 60 million yen. This figure is prohibitive, although land prices have plunged after the "bubble economy" in the late 80's and the early 90's. Houses for sale are scarce in urban areas, where in terms of both prices and availability, it is difficult to buy a home.

The ratio of owned houses to the total houses was 60% in 1993, which was 2% lower than in 1983. This ratio is expected to decrease from now on.

• How much does it cost to rent an apartment in a convenient location in Tōkyō?

It depends on the size and location of the room, but the rent for a small studio or one-bedroom apartment for one person, located within a 30 to 40-minute commuting radius, starts at 60,000 yen a month.

If the room is larger or closer to a train station, the rent will go up to 80,000 yen, and even to 100,000 yen for a sunny room in a good environment.

Old apartments with no baths or showers can be rented for about half the above prices.

When renting an apartment, it is often neccessary to pay five or six months worth of rent as deposit and key money. Usually, a two-months rent deposit, one to two months rent for key money, and a one-month broker fee to the realtor is necessary.

The deposit will be returned to the rentor when he or she

すクリーニング代を引かれて返金されます。

Q: 寝る時，現代では畳の上の布団(ふとん)派とベッド派，どっちが多いですか？

布団派です。ベッドメーカーのフランスベッドが1994年に行った調査では，ベッドを使っている世帯は全体の53.1%もありますが，人口比率で見ると27.0%でした。つまり，ベッドのある家は2軒に1軒なのですが，ベッドで寝ている人は3，4人に1人ということになります。

日本でベッドが使用されたのは病院や軍隊が最初です。その後，ホテルの出現によってベッドがポピュラーになりました。

Q: 日本のトイレは「座る」式，「しゃがむ」式，どっちが多いですか？

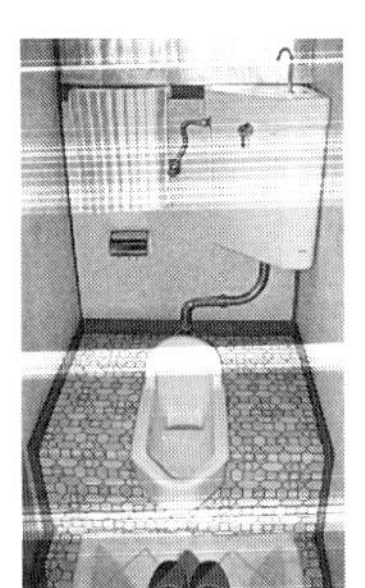
Squatting-style toilet

衛生陶器工業会の発表によれば，1994年に出荷された便器のうち89%が洋式，つまり「座る」式です。これは新規に設置された便器の割合ですから，次第に「座る」式が多くなっていることは事実です。

洋式便器は明治時代（1870年頃）に日本に入ってきましたが，急速に普及したのはこの20－30年のことです。

「座る」式が増えた理由は，一つには大小兼用にできるので，スペースを節約できること。また，しゃがんで力むよりは楽なので，お年寄りには心配がないことなどです。

ちなみに，ホテルやレストランなどでは洋式トイレが多く，駅や公園などにある公衆トイレでは和式が圧倒的に多いようです。

moves out, minus the fee for cleaning up the room.

• Which is more popular in Japanese bedrooms, *futon* on *tatami* mats or western beds?

*Futon*s. According to a survey conducted by France Bed, a bed manufacturer, 53.1% of Japanese households use beds, however, in comparison to the ratio of total population, the figure was 27.0%. Put in another way, every two households own a bed, but only one out of three or four people sleep on the bed.

In Japan, beds were first used in hospitals and by the military. They later became popular when western-style hotels were built.

• Which type of toilet is the more common, the Western-style sit-down type or the traditional squatting type?

According to a Sanitary Ceramics Industry report, 89% of the toilet bowls shipped out of factories in 1994 were western-style, sit-down types. This figure reflects the number of newly installed toilets, which indicates that sit-down types are on the increase.

Western-style toilets were introduced to Japan around 1870 and they have quickly gained popularity in the past twenty to thirty years.

The increase of sit-down types is due to its economy of space, since they make urinals unnecessary. It is also easier to use in that one does not have to squat, which is a feature particularly welcomed by seniors.

For example, hotels and restaurants have more western-style sit-on toilets, while public toilets (like those in stations and parks) have more of the Japanese squatting-style.

7

生活と習慣

日本の祝休日・祭り

Q: 日本にはどんな国民の休日がありますか？

法律で定められている祝休日は，現在，15あります。その祝休日が日曜日と重なったときには，翌日の月曜日が休みになります。

元旦（がんたん）　1月1日

多くの会社が，年末から1月4日までを休みにします。

成人の日　1月15日

前年の4月2日からその年の4月1日までに20歳に達したすべての青年たちを祝う日。

建国記念の日　2月11日

日本書紀で神武（じんむ）天皇が即位したと言われる日を太陽暦に換算した日。

春分の日　3月21日ごろ

7

LIFE AND CUSTOMS

Japanese Holidays and Festivals

• What are the national holidays in Japan?

There are 15 national holidays determined by law. When a holiday falls on a Sunday, the following Monday substitutes for the holiday.

New Year's Day January 1

Many offices are closed from the last day of the year through January 4.

Coming-of-Age Day January 15

A day to celebrate the coming of age of all the youths who have attained the age of twenty.

National Foundation Day Februrary 11

The day of the first Emperor Jinmu's enthronement, as written in the *Nihon Shoki*. The date is based on the solar calendar.

Vernal Equinox Day around March 21

太陽が春分点を通過する日。自然をたたえ，生物をいつくしむ日。

緑の日 4月29日

昭和天皇の誕生日だった日。崩御(ほうぎょ)の後，日本の緑を守る日とされました。

憲法記念日 5月3日

1947年，日本国憲法が施行された日を記念する日。

国民の休日 5月4日

これは特別な祝日ではないのですが，3日と5日にはさまれているので作られた休日です。

子供の日 5月5日

子供の健康，幸福を願う日。昔は「端午(たんご)の節句」と言って，男の子の成長を祝う日でした。鯉のぼりを立てます。

海の日 7月20日

海の恩恵に感謝する日

敬老の日 9月15日

年配の人たちに敬意を表する日。1966年に制定されました。

秋分の日 9月23日か24日

太陽が秋分点を通過する日。祖先をうやまい，亡くなった人々をしのぶ日です。

体育の日 10月10日

1964年の東京オリンピックの開会の日を記

A day when the sun passes the vernal equinox. It is a day to celebrate nature and living things.

Greenery Day April 29

The late Emperor Showa's birthday. After his death, it was designated as a day for preserving Japan's greenery.

Constitution Day May 3

A day to commemorate the enactment of the Constitution of Japan in 1947.

National Holiday May 4

It was decided that this day should be a national holiday because it is between May 3, Constitution Day, and May 5, Children's day.

Children's Day May 5

A day to wish for the health and happiness of children. It used to be called *tango no sekku*, a day of celebration for boys only. Carp-shaped streamers are flown on this day.

Marine Day July 20

A day to thank the sea for its blessings.

Respect-for-the-Aged Day September 15

A day to show respect to the elderly, enacted in 1966.

Autumnal Equinox Day September 23 or 24

The day when the sun passes the autumnal equinox. It is a day to remember the dead and to show respect to one's ancestors.

Health-Sports Day October 10

Enacted in 1966 in commemoration of the opening of the

念して1966年に定められた日。健康を奨励する日です。

文化の日 11月3日

1946年，日本国憲法が公布された日を記念して定められたもので，日本の文化の振興を考える日とされています。

勤労感謝の日 11月23日

勤労に感謝をし，収穫を祝う日。昔は「新嘗祭（にいなめさい）」と言って，新しく収穫した穀物を神に捧げて感謝をした日から由来しています。

天皇誕生日 12月23日

現在の天皇の誕生を祝う日。天皇が存命の間続けられます。

Q: 正月には何をしますか？

Kadomatsu

1年の初めに当たる正月は，本来は収穫をつかさどる神や，一族を守る祖先の霊を迎える年中行事です。門松やしめ飾りは，その神を迎えるためのものです。丸いお餅を2つ重ねた鏡餅は神さまが食べる食べ物です。

子供に「お年玉」，たいていはお金をあげますが，これは神様が「お前たちもがんばれ」と授けてくれるもの，というのが趣旨です。

Q: 節分とは何ですか？

立春の前の日に行われる行事です。立春は2月3日か4日です。家の戸を開け，「鬼は外，福は内」と叫びながら煎った大豆を投げ，悪鬼や悪運を家から追い払います。

1964 Tokyo Olympics, it is a day to promote health.

Culture Day November 3

A day to promote cultural prosperity of Japan, enacted in commemoration of the day when the Constitution of Japan was promulgated in 1946.

Labor Thanksgiving Day November 23

A day to appreciate labor and to celebrate a good harvest. It used to be called *niiname sai*, when new crops were offered to the gods with gratitude.

The Emperor's Birthday December 23

The current Emperor's birthday. It will be celebrated while the Emperor is alive.

• What do the Japanese do during the New Year holidays?

January is the start of the new year. It originally was an annual event to welcome the god of harvest and the spirits of ancestors who protect their families. *Kadomatsu* (gate pines) and *shimekazari* (sacred rope), both decorations for the New Year, are prepared to invite the gods of harvest, and *kagami-mochi*, two pieces of round rice cake one on top of the other, is offered.

Children are given *otoshidama* (a New Year's present) by adults, in most cases money, and it is meant to be a gift from the gods to encourage children to do their best.

• What is *setsubun*?

Setsubun is held one day before the first day of spring, which is February 3rd or 4th. People open the doors of their houses and drive the demons, or bad luck, out of their homes by throwing soybeans and shouting "Demons out! Good luck in!"

そもそもは宮中で大晦日に行われたもので，悪鬼を追い払って新年を迎えたのです。この風習に，田植えの行事に豆を投げるという固有の民間の風習が重なりあって，今の形になったようです。

Q: 桃の節句，雛(ひな)祭りとは何ですか？

Hina ningyō

3月3日に行われる，女の子の誕生を祝い，これからの幸せを願う祭りです。雛祭には，昔の衣装を着せた雛人形に桃の花をそえて飾って，白酒という米で作った甘い飲み物を供えます。

そもそもは，水辺で体を清める風習でしたが，代わりに紙人形を使うことになり，その後，江戸時代になって，その人形が「雛人形」として工夫されるようになりました。

Q: お彼岸というのは何ですか？

仏教の行事ですが，日本だけに生まれた習慣です。春分の日の前後3日間を「春の彼岸」，秋分の日の前後3日間を「秋の彼岸」と言います。寒さ・暑さが切り替わる時です。祖先を供養する日で，墓参りに行き，花やお萩という食べ物を供えたりします。

Q: お花見はいつから始まりましたか？

日本人の花と言えば，桜と言われるほどです。パッと咲いた花の下で，桜を見ながら飲み食いを楽しむという風習が庶民の間に行き渡ったのは，江戸時代になってからのようです。

東京の上野公園のような桜の名所がたくさん

It was started originally as an imperial event on New Year's Eve, for the purpose of getting rid of demons to welcome a happy New Year. Later it was mixed with the indigenous custom of throwing soybeans at the time of planting rice seedlings, and it has thus turned into the present custom.

• What is *hinamatsuri*?

It is the girls' festival on March 3, when the birth of girls is celebrated and wishes are expressed for their future happiness. *Hinamatsuri* is the day on which *hina ningyō*, a set of dolls dressed in ancient costumes, are displayed together with peach blossoms as decoration. A sweet drink made of rice called *shirozake* is offered.

The original form of this custom was purifying oneself in water, but later paper dolls were used instead of people bathing themselves. In the Edo period (1600–1868), paper dolls were turned into more sophisticated ones, now called *hina ningyō*.

• What is *higan*?

Higan is a Buddhist event peculiar to Japan. Three days before and after vernal equinox is called spring *higan* and three days before and after autumnal equinox is called autumn *higan*. Both *higan* is the time of seasonal changes. On these occasions people visit their ancestors' graves and offer flowers and sweets called *ohagi*.

• When did the custom of flower viewing start?

The favorite flower of the Japanese is the cherry blossom. While viewing cherry blossoms in full bloom, people enjoy eating and drinking. It was in the Edo period (1600–1868) that this custom called *hanami* became popular.

There are many places known for their beautiful cherry

あり，そんな所では，かなり前から飲み食いの場所を確保しようとして争う光景も見られます。

Q: 花祭りとは何をする祭りですか？

4月8日の釈迦の誕生を祝う日です。正式には「灌仏会」と言います。釈迦の誕生のときに，竜が天から舞い降りてきて香水を注いだ，という故事に基づいて，釈迦の像に甘茶を注ぎます。

Q: 端午の節句とは何ですか？

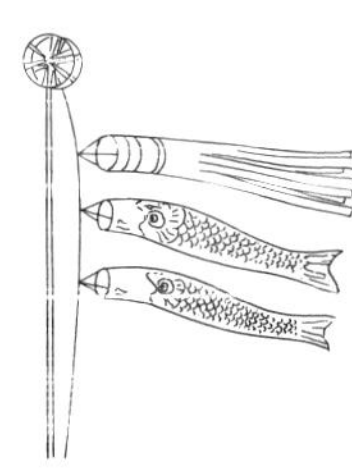

Carp-shaped streamers

5月5日の「子供の日」に昔から行われていた行事です。家の外に鯉のぼりを立て，武者人形を飾って，男の子のすこやかな成長を祝います。

この習慣は武家社会で発展したものですが，民間ではこの日に，女性が先に風呂に入るとか，男が食事を用意するなどの女性上位の習慣があり，昔は男の子の祭りというだけではありませんでした。

Q: 七夕とはどんな日ですか？

7月7日の夜，天の川をはさんで牽牛星と織女星が年に1度会う，という伝説にちなんだ行事です。

中国から伝わったもので，日本の宮中に入り，次第に民衆の間に広まりました。短冊に願いを書いて，庭に立てた竹の枝に結びつけます。

blossoms including Ueno Park in Tōkyō, where people compete to keep spaces for their parties well in advance.

• What do people do in *hanamatsuri* (Flower Festival)?

Hanamatsuri on April 8 is the festival to celebrate the birth of Gautama Buddha. Formally called *kanbutsu-e*, the festival is observed based on the episode about Buddha's birth, in which a dragon flew down from heaven and poured fragrant water. People now pour *amacha*, or sweetened tea, onto the statue of Buddha.

• What is *tango no sekku*?

This is an event handed down from ancient times which is held on May 5, Children's Day. People express hope that each boy in the family will grow up healthy and strong by flying carp-shaped streamers outside the house and displaying a warrior doll.

This custom developed in the warrior class society in the feudal era, but the event was also observed among civilians at the time in a different way. Women were made superior to men on that day; for example, women took a bath before men and men prepared meals for women.

• What does the *tanabata* festival celebrate?

Tanabata, the Star Festival, is the event based on the legend in which two lovers, *Kengyū* (the star Altair) and *Shokujo* (Vega), who were separated by the Milky Way, meet just once a year on the night of July 7.

Originally from China and modified into a Japanese style, the event spread from the imperial palace to ordinary people. Bamboo branches are set up in the garden and decorated with strips of paper on which people write their wishes.

Q: 盆(盂蘭盆)とは何ですか?

盆は本来は旧暦の7月半ばに行われましたが，今は7月13–16日，地方によっては8月13–16日に行われます。

盆は家に帰ってくる祖先の霊を迎える仏教の行事です。13日に祖先の霊を迎え入れる火をたき，16日の夜にまた火をたいて，霊をあの世に送ります。

Q: 月見には何をしますか?

9月の中旬の満月を「中秋の名月」と呼びます。この月を観賞するのが月見です。もとは中国の風習でしたが，平安時代から日本でも行われるようになっています。

団子を作り，畑の作物といっしょに供え，ススキを飾って月を観賞します。月見の供え物は，盗んでもかまわない，という習慣の地方もあります。

Q: 七五三とはどんな祝いごとですか?

Shichi-go-san

親が子供の成長を祝う行事です。男の子は3歳と5歳，女の子は3歳と7歳になった年の11月15日に，氏神様に連れて行き，子供たちの将来を祈ります。

男の子は羽織(はおり)にはかま，女の子は着物に着飾って神社に行きます。最近はスーツやドレスなどを着ている子もいます。

Q: 大晦日(おおみそか)には何をしますか?

正月を迎える大晦日は，1年の区切りをつけ，きたるべき年に備えるための重要な日です。昔

• What is *Bon* (*Urabon*)?

Originally celebrated in mid-July according to the lunar calendar, *Bon*, the Festival of Souls, is now held from July 13 to 16, or from August 13 to 16, depending on the area.

It is a Buddhist festival in honor of the spirits of the dead who return to their families. On the first day, spirits of ancestors are welcomed by an open-air fire, and on the night of the last day another open-air fire is made to see them off to the other world.

• What do people do on *tsukimi*?

Tsukimi, which means moon-gazing, is the custom to appreciate the full moon in mid-September called *chūshū no meigetsu*. Introduced from China, the custom spread through Japan in the Heian period (794–1192).

Dango, a kind of dumplings, together with crops from fields, were offered to the moon. Japanese pampas grass are decorated, while people sit and appreciate the beauty of the moon. In some regions people are allowed to steal the offerings.

• What does *shichi-go-san* celebrate?

It is an event in which parents celebrate their children's growth. On November 15, 3 and 5-year-old boys, and 3 and 7-year-old girls are taken to shrines, where their parents pray for their future.

Boys often wear *haori*, or half-coat, and *hakama*, or divided skirt, and girls wear *kimono*. Some children wear suits or dresses.

• What do people do on New Year's Eve?

New Year's Eve is an important day in that it is the day to wrap up the old year and start preparing for the coming year.

は正月の準備も大変で，餅をついたり，正月の間の食事としてお節(せち)料理を用意したり，主婦は大忙しでした。しかし今は，できあいを買ってきて済ませるという家庭も多くなりました。

大晦日の夜は，正月の準備を終え，一家が揃って食事をし，除夜の鐘を聞き，元日の朝まで起きていたのが普通でした。地方によっては，大晦日に寝ると白髪になる，と言い伝えられていたところもあります。

Q: 日本人にとって祭りとは何ですか？

語源の「マツ」には，見えないものが見えるところに来るのを歓待する，という意味があります。

つまり，日ごろ目には見えない神様が来てくれるわけで，その神様を歓待するのが祭りというわけです。日本各地に伝承されている祭りは，基本的に神々と人の交流という形で行われています。

ただし，無数の神様の中には病気や自然災害をもたらす神もあり，こうした災厄の神を追放するのも祭りです。

Q: 日本の三大祭りと言われるものは何ですか？

Gion Festival

日本人は“3”という数字で物事を一くくりにするのが大好きです。しかし，祭りについて3つを挙げるとなると説が分かれます。

たとえば，東京の三社祭り，京都の祇園(ぎおん)祭り，大阪の天神祭りの3つという説，東京の山王(さんのう)祭り，京都の葵(あおい)祭り，大阪の天神祭りの３つという説などです。

Decades ago, preparation for the New Year kept people very busy making rice cake and special New Year dishes called *o-sechi*, but nowadays many households buy them at stores.

At that time it was cutomary for a family to have dinner together after they had finished preparing for the New Year. They listened to *joya no kane*, or the watch-night bell starting at midnight, and stayed awake till the morning of the New Year. In some regions there was a saying that one's hair turns gray if one sleeps on New Year's Eve.

• What is the significance of festivals for the Japanese?

Matsu, the original meaning of the word *matsuri* (festivals) in Japanese, means "to welcome the invisible to a place where they became visible."

In other words, gods, who are usually invisible, visit during festivals, and are welcomed by the people. Japanese festivals handed down from ancient times are basically celebrated to bring about communication between gods and people.

Among the myriads of gods, however, there are some that bring about diseases and natural disasters, so festivals are also set up to ward off evil gods.

• What are the three largest festivals in Japan?

The Japanese like to use the number 3 to summarize things, but as far as festivals are concerned, opinions are divided on which three to choose.

For instance, there is a view that the Sanja Festival in Tōkyō, the Gion Festival in Kyōto, and the Tenjin Festival in Ōsaka are the three largest festivals. But another view holds that the three largest festivals are the Sannō Festival in Tōkyō,

また各地域ごとに，東北三大祭り（青森ねぶた祭り，秋田竿灯（かんとう）祭り，仙台の七夕祭り）とか，京都三大祭り（葵祭り，祇園祭り，時代祭り）などとも言ったりします。

日本の結婚

Q：日本ではどんな結婚式が一般的ですか？

Bride and groom

日本の結婚式は，神前結婚式が7割と言われていますが，ほかにキリスト教式，仏式などで行うのが一般的です。いずれも信仰にはあまり関わりがないのが特徴です。

昔は，結婚式は嫁入り先の家で行ったものですが，明治時代になって，神社での結婚式が行われるようになりました。

教会での結婚式は信者に限るのが原則ですが，事前にオリエンテーションを受ければ式を挙げられる教会があります。

神社や教会に行かなくても，神主や牧師が出張してきて，ホテルや結婚式場に作られた祭壇の前でできます。

いずれの場合も，挙式のあとは記念撮影をして披露宴となります。披露宴は，お世話になっている人や親しい人たちを招いて，結婚したことをお披露目する祝宴です。

Q：結婚式にはいくらぐらいかかりますか？

三和銀行が1992年に行った調査によれば，挙式・披露宴にかかる平均費用は296万6000

Aoi Festival in Kyōto, and the Tenjin Festival in Ōsaka.

Each region has its three largest festivals. In the Tōhoku region, Nebuta Festival in Aomori, the Kantō Festival in Akita, and the Tanabata Festival in Sendai are said to be the largest three. In Kyōto there are the Aoi Festival, the Gion Festival, and the Jidai Festival.

Japanese Marriages

• What is the most common wedding ceremony like in Japan?

About 70% of Japanese weddings are conducted in *Shintō* style, and the rest are conducted according to Christian, Buddhist, or other style. Most couples do not associate their chosen styles of weddings with religious faith.

In olden times the wedding ceremony was held in the husband's home. Ceremonies in shrines became common in the Meiji period (1868–1912).

Christian-style ceremonies in churches are usually open only to Christians, but recently some churches admit couples who take classes on Christianity.

Hotels and wedding halls have facilities for both *Shintō*-style and Christian-style ceremonies, where *Shintō* priests and ministers come to preside over the ceremonies.

After the ceremonies, commemorative photos are taken and wedding receptions are held. A wedding reception is an event to make the couple's marriage public, to which friends and acquaintances are invited.

• How much does it cost to hold a wedding?

A 1992 survey by Sanwa Bank showed that the average cost of a wedding ceremony and reception is 2,966,000 yen,

円。新郎・新婦や仲人を含めた出席者数の平均は81人なので，出席者1人当たり3，4万円というのが1つの目安です。

結婚は，結婚する当人たちだけでなく，家と家の結びつきでもありますから，世間に恥ずかしいことはできず，豪華な披露宴が多くなりました。

しかし，“自分たちらしさ”を出したユニークな結婚式をしたいという人が増えており，結婚式のスタイルも少しずつ変わってきました。

Q: 日本人の結婚の平均年齢はいくつですか？

厚生省の人口動態統計によれば，1993年に結婚した男性の平均年齢は29.7歳，女性は27.1歳となっています。ただし，これは全婚姻の平均で，初婚だけに限ると男性は28.4歳，女性は26.1歳です。

15歳から29歳までの女性で結婚している人の割合は10%を切るという調査（読売新聞読者調査 1995年）もあります。

結婚する女性の平均年齢が25歳以下だったのは1970年代前半までで，男女ともに日本人の結婚年齢は高くなっており，結婚する年齢の幅も大きく広がってきました。

Q: どれくらいの人が離婚していますか？

厚生省の人口動態統計によれば，1993年の離婚件数は約19万件。結婚したのは約80万件ですから，4組のうち1組は離婚したことになります。離婚したカップルの婚姻期間は平均10.1年です。

離婚件数は増加する一方で，「バツイチ」とか「成田離婚」，「熟年離婚」などという新しい言葉

and the average number of people attending the reception including the bride, bridegroom, and go-between is 81. That means it costs 30,000 to 40,000 yen per person.

Marriage is considered to tie not only the couple, but also the families of the couple. Many families hold luxurious weddings to make themselves look respectable to the world.

However, the style of weddings has gradually changed as more people express a desire to hold unique weddings suitable to them.

• What is the average age of marriage of the Japanese?

According to the 1993 Statistics of Population Movement by the Ministry of Health and Welfare, the average age of marrige for men is 29.7 and 27.1 for women. These figures are the average for all marriages; for people who marry for the first time, the average is 28.4 years for men, and 26.1 for women.

A 1995 Yomiuri Shimbun readers' survey reveals that less than 10% of women between 15 and 29 are married.

Until the early 1970's, the average age of marriage of women was less than 25, but it is getting higher for both men and women, and people are getting married at a wider range of ages.

• What is the divorce rate?

Statistics compiled by the Ministry of Health and Welfare show that the number of divorces was about 190,000 out of 800,000 marriages in 1993, which means one in every 4 couples divorced. The average duration of marriage for the divorced couples was 10.1 years.

The number of divorces has increased greatly, and the trend gave birth to new words, such as *batsu-ichi* (one-time

も生まれました。

バツイチは「離婚経験1回」という意味の言葉の短縮語です。しかし，特に揶揄するような意味合いはなく，「わたし，バツイチよ」と平気で口にする女性もいます。

成田離婚は，新婚旅行から帰ってすぐに離婚すること。日本では新婚旅行に海外を選ぶ人が多いのですが，パッとのぼせて結婚したものの，新婚旅行中に興ざめとなり，成田空港に帰り着くころには離婚を決めているカップルもいるのだそうです。

また，熟年離婚は長年連れ添った夫婦が離婚することを言います。長年，結婚生活に耐えて夫に尽くしてきた妻が自由になりたいと言い出すケースです。多くの場合，夫の定年などを機に，離婚をしたいと妻が言い出します。

Q：離婚の慰謝料はどれくらいもらえますか？

1991年度の司法統計年報によれば，慰謝料の平均支払い額は435万7000円となっています。ただし，これは家庭裁判所の調停によって成立した離婚のうち，慰謝料の支払いがあったケースの平均金額です。日本では90%以上が協議離婚なので，この数字には含まれていない部分がかなりあります。

結婚していた期間や相手の経済力，離婚の原因などが慰謝料の額を決める要因になります。

なお，子供の養育費は，1人なら月額3万円，2人なら月額5万円という数字を聞きますが，これも相手の経済力によります。

cross), *Narita rikon* (Narita divorce), and *jukunen rikon* (mature-age divorce).

Batsu-ichi refers to people who have divorced once, but it does not have so much of a derogatory connotation. Some women openly admit they are *batsu-ichi*.

Narita rikon means to divorce immediately after the couple have returned from their honeymoon. Many Japanese couples choose foreign countries as their honeymoon destination, but some of them find their love cooling down during the trip and decide to divorce by the time they arrive at Narita Airport.

The word *jukunen rikon* is used when a couple who have been married for many years seek a divorce. Some cases of *jukunen rikon* involve wives who want to be liberated after enduring the marriage and devoting their lives to their husbands for a long time. Many such wives express their wish for a divorce taking advantage of their husbands' retirement.

• How much is the average alimony for a divorce?

The 1991 Yearbook of Judicial Statistics shows that the average alimony payment is 4,357,000 yen, which is the average amount incurred in divorce cases settled in the family court. Since more than 90% of Japanese divorces are not settled in court but by mutual agreement, the above average does not apply to the vast majority of divorces.

Deciding factors of the alimony are the duration of marriage, financial capabilities of divorcees, causes of divorces, etc.

A typical amount of alimony paid for children is said to be 30,000 yen a month for one child, and 50,000 yen for two children, but it depends on the payer's financial capabilities.

Q: 国際結婚する人は毎年どれくらいいますか？

厚生省の人口動態統計によれば，1993年に結婚したカップルのうち，夫が日本人で妻が外国人というケースは2万92組，逆は6565組でした。

日本人男性が外国の女性と結婚するケースは，この10年で約5倍に増えています。

国別に見ると，妻が外国人の場合は韓国が最も多くて全体の25.2%，次が中国の23.4%，後はさまざまです。

夫が外国人の場合は，これもトップは韓国で42.1%，ついで米国の21.0%，中国の11.7%となっています。

日本の葬式

Q: どんな葬式をするのが普通ですか？

Incense offering

特に信仰している宗教がなければ，多くの場合，日本の葬式は，仏式で行われます。

亡くなると，普通は家で通夜を行います。通夜は，遺族や近親者がロウソクや線香を絶やさずに，終夜，遺体を守ることです。

そして，翌日以降に，家か寺院で葬式を行います。葬式の段取りなどは，予算や故人の希望に合わせて，葬儀社に任せて行うのが普通です。

葬式は，故人の成仏を祈る葬儀，最後の別れを告げる告別式，と続きます。葬儀では遺体

• How many international marriages are registered every year?

The Health and Welfare Ministry's Statistics of Population Movement show that, among the couples who got married in 1993, the number of couples consisting of a Japanese husband and a foreign wife was 20,092, and the number of couples consisting of a foreign husband and a Japanese wife was 6,565.

The number of cases where Japanese men marry foreign women has quintupled during the past 10 years.

According to their nationalities, Korean wives constitute 25.2% of foreign wives, and 23.4% are Chinese.

42.1% of foreign husbands are Koreans, 21.0% are Americans, and 11.7% are Chinese.

Funerals in Japan

• What is the most common type of funeral?

Most of the funeral services in Japan are administered according to Buddhist rites if there is no specific religion of the deceased.

After a person's death, a wake is held usually at his or her house. A wake is an occasion when the surviving family and close relatives keep a night watch over the corpse, while candles are lit and incense sticks are offered.

During one of the following days, a funeral is held either at the home or a temple. Ordinarily a funeral home takes care of the funeral according to the family's budget and the wishes of the deceased.

A funeral consists of a service in which prayers for the deceased are offered and a farewell ceremony in which atten-

を納棺して祭壇に飾り，僧侶の読経を聞いて親族とごく親しい人が焼香（抹香をたくこと）します。

一般の会葬者は告別式で焼香します。告別式のあと，通常は遺体を火葬場に運びます。

Q：葬式にはいくらぐらいかかりますか？

全日本葬祭業協同組合連合会の調べ（1991年）によれば，会葬者が200人程度の平均的な葬式にかかる費用は，首都圏で202万－206万円，名古屋で127万円，大阪で176万－182万円となっています。

内訳は，葬儀社への支払いが全体の50－60%，参列者の飲食費が20%前後，寺院への支払いが20－30%です。葬儀費用の総額は喪主の月収の3－5倍にもなるものです。

葬儀には，個人にゆかりの友人，縁者，知人から香典が届きますので，葬儀の費用の一部に当てられますが，香典をくれた方には香典返しといって，お返しをしなければなりません。

なお，お墓にかかる費用は200万－300万円，仏壇は20万－50万円もかかります。死ぬのは仕方ないとして遺族の負担は大変です！

Q：香典はいくら持っていくのが常識ですか？

故人の立場やつきあいの程度にもよりますが，普通のつき合いの程度であれば5千円から1万円が一般的です。不祝儀袋に入れ，地味な色のふくさ（のし袋を包む小さな布）や風呂敷に包んで，通夜や告別式に持参します。この場合，新札は避けます。

dants part from the dead. In the funeral service, the coffin is placed on the alter and the priest chants a sutra while relatives and close friends offer incense.

Other attendants offer incense in the farewell ceremony after which the corpse is carried to the crematory.

• How much does a funeral cost?

A 1991 survey by the All Japan Funeral Services Cooperative Union shows that the cost of a typical funeral with 200 attendants is 2.02 to 2.06 million yen in the metropolitan area, 1.27 million yen in Nagoya, and 1.76 to 1.82 million yen in Ōsaka.

About 50 to 60% of the money is paid to the funeral home, about 20% is for the expenses of foods and drinks, and about 20 to 30% goes to the temple. The total cost of a funeral is often equivalent to three to five times the monthly salary of the chief mourner.

Friends, relatives and acquaintances of the deceased provide monetary offerings which can be appropriated for part of the funeral expenses, but the mourner has to return something to them as a token of gratitude.

In addition, it costs 2 to 3 million yen to set up a grave, and a typical Buddhist family alter costs 200,000 to 500,000 yen. The surviving family has to shoulder a large financial burden.

• How much money do people generally offer at funerals?

It all depends on how close one was to the deceased, but aquaintances generally give 5,000 to 10,000 yen enclosed in a special envelope and wrapped in a piece of cloth of subdued color at a wake or a farewell ceremony. New bills are avoided on this occasion.

Q: 日本では必ず火葬にするのですか?

日本では公衆衛生上，地方自治体の条例で土葬を禁止しているところが大半です。イスラム教など，宗教上の理由で土葬を希望する場合は，許可される公営墓地もあります。

日本で外国人が亡くなった場合は，身元が分かれば警察から大使館や関係者に連絡されます。関係者に遺体が引き取られれば，日本での埋葬許可を受けることもできますし，母国に遺体を移送することも可能です。

遺体の引き取り手がない場合は，区市町村長が葬儀をして火葬などを行います。

日本人の余暇・娯楽

Q: 日本人は余暇にはどんなことをして過ごしますか?

日本人が余暇に，どんなことを，1年間に何回ぐらいやったか，というデータ(レジャー白書'94)があります。

音楽観賞	68.4回
体操	50.7回
ジョギング・マラソン	37.9回
園芸・庭いじり	37.5回
ビデオ観賞	21.8回

以下，外食，キャッチボールや野球，バー・スナック・パブ，水泳，トランプ，ドライブ，カラオケ，ピクニック・ハイキング，ボウリングと続きます。これは年齢と性別なしでまとめた数字で，日本の典型的な家族の余暇の過ごし方を表していると言えます。

• Do the Japanese always cremate the dead?

In Japan, most municipal ordinances prohibit burial for public hygenic reasons. Some cemeteries permit upon request, people who wish to be buried because of their religious faith such as Islam.

A foreigner's death in Japan is reported by the police to the embassy and related people when he or she is identified. Once the surviving family receives the corpse, they can either request burial permission or transport the dead to his or her country.

In case there is no one to receive the corpse, the chief of the municipality takes care of the funeral.

Leisure Time and Recreation of the Japanese

• How do the Japanese spend their leisure time?

The 1994 Leisure White Paper provides data on what people of all ages surveyed did in their leisure time, and how many times a year they enjoyed their chosen recreation or pastime.

Listening to music	68.4 times
Physical exercise	50.7 times
Jogging	37.9 times
Gardening	37.5 times
Watching videos	21.8 times

Other activities include eating out, baseball, going to bars, swimming, playing cards, driving, *karaoke*, picnics, hiking, and bowling, in order of popularity. This survey did not consider age and sex and shows how a typical Japanese family spend their leisure time.

金額の上で見ると，回数は3回ですが，やはり国内観光旅行がトップです。次いで，バー・スナックなどでの遊興，そして，外食，ドライブが続いています。しかし，全体的には，金のかかることは敬遠し，身近なところで安く楽しむという時代になってきました。

Q: 子供たちの楽しみは何ですか?

次々に新しいソフトが出るテレビゲームが圧倒的に強いようです。学校が終わっても，塾に行ったり，宿題に追われる彼らには，外を出歩くひまはありません。親の目をかすめて取り組むテレビゲームが，いちばんのスリルでしょう。

それにマンガです。週刊誌，月刊誌の連載物を読むのを，彼らは絶対に欠かしません。

ちなみに，文部省の調査によれば，学習塾に通っている子供の割合が，小学5年生で31%，小学6年生で42%，中学生で60%だそうで，遊ぶひまがないのがかわいそうです。

Q: お父さんたちの楽しみは何ですか?

Golf practice range

働き過ぎの日本のお父さんたちには，同僚との仕事帰りの一杯が楽しみ，という人が，まだまだたくさんいます。そして，休みの日にはゴルフ，何もしないときは昼寝……という人も多いでしょう。

しかし，世の中全体としては，週休2日となり，労働時間が短縮されてきて，余暇が多くなってきましたので，余暇の時間を自己の啓発，健康づくりのための活動，また，ボランティア活動などに使いたいという人たちがどんどん増えています。

In terms of money spent, domestic trips rank first, although only an average of three trips are made in a year, followed by drinking in bars, eating out, and driving. Inexpensive recreation available to anyone is becoming more and more popular these days.

• What do children enjoy doing?

An overwhelmingly popular recreation among children is video games, for which new software is issued one after another. Many children cannot afford much time to play, especially outside after school because of *juku*, a cram school or homework. It is a thrill for children to play video games without their parent's knowledge.

Reading *manga* (comic books) is another pastime the majority of children enjoy. They always look forward to reading serialized *manga* in weekly and monthly magazines.

A survey by the Ministry of Education shows that the ratio of children going to cram schools, is 31% for fifth grade students, 42% for sixth grade students, and 60% for junior high school students. It is a pity that children have no time to play.

• What do men enjoy?

Many Japanese male salaried workers, who are often described as workaholic, find their pleasure in having a drink with their colleagues after work. On holidays some play golf, and others just relax and take a nap.

With the overall trend of having more leisure time because of two-day weekends and less working hours, more and more people want to make the most of their free time by getting involved in self-development, health activities, and volunteer activities.

Q: パチンコはいつごろ日本に誕生したのですか？

パチンコの原型は1920年代にアメリカから伝わったコリントゲームです。これが，1925年に改良され，大人のための遊びになります。そして戦後，たくさんの台を並べ，景品を付けたことにより一気に人気が出ました。

玉をはじく方式も，指ではじく方式から電動式になり，今では，玉の出方はコンピュータで制御されています。

中央に示された絵や数字が一致すると，大当たりで多数の玉が出るようにし，ギャンブル的な性格を強くしたこと，景品を裏で現金に代える組織があることなどが，パチンコの人気を急激に上げたと言われます。

最近は店構えもしゃれてきて，景品にブランド物を置き，女性の客も引きつけています。1995年のパチンコ産業の総売上げは26兆円を超え，今や自動車産業をしのいでいるのです。

Q: 囲碁の魅力はどこにありますか？

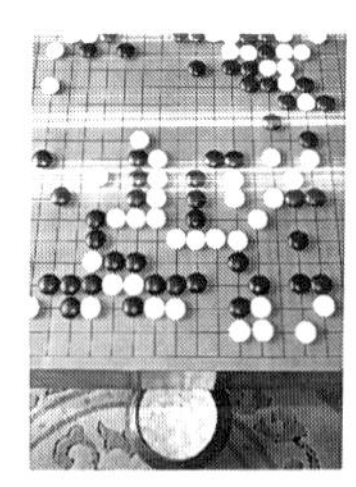

Go

囲碁は古く中国に発したゲームです。ルールは単純ですが，なかなか奥行きが深いのです。

碁盤の目は縦横それぞれ19の線の，361の交点で示されます。2人のプレーヤーが，この361箇所に交互に白と黒の石を置いて，相手よりも多い地を確保する勝負です。ゲームによって石の置き方は千差万別で，あっという間に大逆転されることもあります。

• When was *pachinko*, or vertical pinball game, born in Japan?

The original form of *pachinko* is the Corinthian game introduced from the United States in the 1920's. The game was modified into *pachinko* in 1925, and after World War II, it instantly gained immense popularity by offering prizes.

In the course of development, the manually-operated system of striking balls was improved to electrically-powered system and now the ball distribution is controlled by computers.

Some of the reasons why *pachinko* has become so popular are that it has stimulated gambling characteristics by adding features like slot machines, and that there are underground organizations which provide services to exchange prizes for cash.

The latest *pachinko* parlors have become very fashionable in their decor and offer name-brand products as prizes, attracting female customers. The industry's total sales exceeded 26 trillion yen in 1995, which surpassed the sales of the automobile industry.

• What is attractive about *go*?

Go originally developed in ancient times in China. Though its rules are simple, *go* provides sophisticated pleasure.

It is played by two players on a square board with 19 vertical lines, 19 horizontal lines, and 361 intersections. The two players alternately place stones of their color, either black or white, and compete in taking stones by surrounding as much territory as possible. The player who takes the most captured territory is the winner. Thousands of tactics exist in the game, and there is always the possibility of a dramatic reversal.

Q: 将棋の魅力はどこにありますか？

Shōgi

将棋のルーツはインドにあり，それが西洋に伝わったものがチェス，日本に伝わったものが将棋です。

ですから駒の働きやルールはチェスと大変よく似ていますが，日本の将棋の特徴は取った相手の駒を自分の駒として再度使用できることです。このためチェスではよく起こる「引き分け」がほとんどなく，白熱した戦いになります。

日本のスポーツ

Q: 日本人が自分で楽しむスポーツは何が人気ですか？

ボウリング，器具を使わない体操，ジョギング，プールでの水泳などが，日常の健康のために人気のあるスポーツです。テニスも幅広い年齢の人が楽しんでいます。

野球は昔は空き地でよく行われていましたが，今は空き地もなく，やりたくてもできなくなりました。若い人に人気があるサッカーやバスケットも，特に都会ではプレーを楽しむ場所が十分にないのが現状です。

ゴルフは，日本にはゴルフ場は多いものの，プレー代が高く，気軽には楽しむことができません。ビジネスの延長の「社用ゴルフ」は，不景気で激減だそうです。

冬になると，かなり多くの人たちがスキーを楽しみます。スノーボードの人気が出てから，スキーに行く人の数はぐんと増えたようです。日本は雪が多い国なのです。

• What is interesting about *shōgi*?

The game of *shōgi* originated in India and became chess in the West and *shōgi* in Japan.

Therefore, the movement of pieces and rules are similar to those of chess, but one characteristic peculiar to *shōgi* is that a player can reuse captured pieces as his or her own. This rule of *shōgi* often generates exciting moments toward the end, with fewer drawn games than chess.

Sports in Japan

• What kind of sports do the Japanese participate in?

For daily exercises for health, bowling, physical exercises, jogging, swimming, and tennis are very popular with people in a wide range of age groups.

Decades ago people used to play baseball in vacant lots, but now it has become almost impossible to do so because there is not much vacant land left. Young people love soccer and basketball, but in urban areas it is very hard to find enough spaces to play.

Although there are numerous golf courses in Japan, the green fee is so prohibitive that not everyone can enjoy this sport. Opportunities to play golf on companies' expense plunged because of the economic recession.

Skiing is the favorite sport of the Japanese in winter. The skiing population in this snowy country has increased as snowboarding has become quite popular.

Q：観戦するスポーツは何が人気ですか？

実際に競技場に観客が押し掛けるスポーツとしては，まずはプロ野球，そして，特に若い人が多いのはJリーグのサッカー，ラグビー，バレーボールです。ラグビーは中高年齢の人にも人気があります。バレーボールには，なぜか，熱狂的な若い女性のファンが目立ちます。

テレビ観戦では，プロ野球，そして大相撲が肩を並べます。次にJリーグのサッカーとプロゴルフのコンペが続きます。

春と夏の2回ある高校野球大会が始まると，日本全国が出身県からの出場校を応援して沸き立ちます。高校生の野球で，これだけ騒ぎ立てる日本の姿は，外国人には異様に見えるそうですね。

Q：相撲は昔から日本の国技だったのですか？

昔，相撲は五穀豊穣（ごこくほうじょう）を占ったり，神意をうかがう神事でした。史実に記録されている最初の相撲は642年のことで，その後，9世紀初めには宮廷の儀式になっていたのです。

12世紀以降，武士が政治の実権をにぎるようになると，相撲は，戦場での実戦的な武術としての性格を持つようになりました。しかし，江戸時代になると，神社の祭礼などにおける興行として行われるようになり，次第に見世物的になっていきました。

Sumō match © JAMP

この相撲を，国技と呼ぶようになったのは明治時代末の20世紀初めからです。国家主義のもとに天皇の神格化が進み，それと共に，元は宮廷の儀式であった相撲が国技化されていき，現在に至っています。

• What sports are popular as spectator sports?

Professional baseball always attracts a large number of spectators. Japan league professional soccer, rugby, and volleyball have a lot of young fans, whereas rugby is popular also with middle-aged people. Young girls make up a greater part of the enthusiastic volleyball fans.

TV viewers love broadcasts of baseball games and *sumō* wrestling bouts most. Broadcasts of J. league soccer games and professional golf tournaments also have high audience ratings.

When the National Senior High School Baseball Championship held in spring and summer begins, the whole nation is heated as people cheer the teams that represents their prefectures. The fact that people make such a fuss over high school baseball games might seem odd to some foreigners.

• Has *sumō* been the national sport from ancient times?

Sumō in ancient times was a sacred event to foretell an abundant harvest and to predict the will of the gods. The oldest bout of *sumō* recorded in history was 642 A.D., and it was adopted as a ritual in the Court in the early 9th century.

After the 12th century, when warriors began holding real power in politics, *sumō* acquired a characteristic of a practical martial art to be used in the battlefield. In the Edo period (1603–1868) *sumō* bouts began to be performed as part of a show in festivities at shrines.

It was not until the end of the Meiji period (1868–1912), or the early 20th century, when *sumō* was mentioned as the national sport for the first time, as the Emperor was deified under the nationalism and *sumō*, a Court ritual, was accepted by the government.

Q: 相撲の世界はどんな世界ですか?

相撲の勝負は，相手を土俵から押し出すか，相手の体のどこかを地に着けさせれば勝ちになります。

力士になるには，50近くある相撲部屋のどれか一つに所属しなければなりません。衣食住のすべてを部屋が面倒を見てくれ，力士になるべく養成されていきます。親方の家族以外はすべて男の世界です。

力士は，その実力によっていくつものランクにわけられています。最下位は序ノ口といい，ここからスタートし，序二段，三段目，幕下，十両，前頭と上がります。その上が小結，関脇，大関で，最高位が横綱です。

十両以上になると関取と呼ばれ，日本相撲協会から月給が出ますが，幕下以下には場所の成績に応じて与えられるわずかな奨励金だけです。

Q: 柔道はいつごろ日本で完成されましたか?

Jūdō

柔道は1882年嘉納治五郎(1860－1938)によって創始されました。

柔道の技の源は柔術に求められます。柔術は，武士が戦場で敵と戦うときのさまざまな技から発展したものです。

嘉納治五郎もこの柔術を習得しますが，そのうちに，単に勝つための柔術に満足することができず，体を鍛え，精神を修養することを目的にした柔道を創り出します。

1882年，東京の永昌寺に最初に講道館を開いたときは，畳数12畳の道場，門人はわずか9

• What is the world of the *sumō* wrestler like?

The winner of *sumō* is decided when the opponent is forced out of the ring (*dohyō*) or when any part of his body touches the ground.

In order to become a *sumō* wrestler, one has to belong to one of the almost 50 *sumō* stables. The stables take care of every aspect of the newcomers' lives including food, clothing, and housing, while training them to be strong wrestlers. It is a man's world except for the family of the stable master.

Wrestlers are ranked according to their ability. The lowest rank is called *jonokuchi*, which is the starting point. There are 9 other ranks such as *jonidan*, *sandanme*, *makushita*, *jūryō*, *maegashira*, *komusubi*, *sekiwake* and *ōzeki*. At the top of the ranks are the *yokozuna*, or grand champions.

Wrestlers above the rank of *jūryō* are called *sekitori* and receive monthly salaries. What the other wrestlers get is just a small amount of incentive depending on their record in tournaments.

• When was *jūdō* established?

Jūdō was established in 1882 by Kanō Jigorō (1860–1938).

The origin of the techniques of the sport can be found in *jūjutsu*, which developed from warrior fighting techniques in the battlefield.

Kanō, who had mastered *jūjutsu*, was not satisfied with fights just for the pupose of winning, and created *jūdō* aiming for both physical and mental strength.

In 1882, Kanō opened Kōdōkan in the Eishōji Temple in Tōkyō, with only 9 students in a 12 *tatami*-mat room as a prac-

人だったといいます。それが今はオリンピック種目にもなりました。

Q: スポーツになった日本古来の武道にはどんなものがありますか？

Kendō

代表的なものを挙げましょう。武具を使わないものとしては，柔術から発展した柔道。そして，中国から伝来して沖縄で発展した空手があります。

剣道は武士の剣術から生まれてきたものです。練習に竹刀（しない）を用い，面や胴当てなどを用いるようになったのは江戸時代からで，このスタイルで競技を行います。

弓道（きゅうどう）も，その起源は昔に遡りますが，弓道という名前が使われるようになったのは，20世紀になってからです。弓道の競技には，近い距離の的を座って射るものと，遠い距離の的を立って射るものの2つがあります。

日本の武道から発生したスポーツの共通した特徴は，礼儀，精神性を重視するところにあります。

Q: 日本のプロ野球のチームはいくつありますか？

セントラルリーグとパシフィックリーグに，それぞれに6チーム，計12チームがあります。

それぞれのチームには二軍があります。チームを東西に分けて，イースタンリーグ，ウエスタンリーグというリーグ戦をしています。

本場のアメリカから，野球が日本に入ってきたのは1931年のことで，1934年に初めて，今のジャイアンツである「大日本東京野球倶楽部」が設立されました。そして，1936年，全部で7チー

tice gym. *Jūdō* is now a world sport and an Olympic event.

• What kind of traditional martial arts of Japan are practiced as sports?

Among traditional Japanese martial arts which are practiced as sports today, *jūdō* and *karate* are the ones in which no armor is used. *Jūdō* developed from *jūjutsu*, and *karate* was introduced from China and developed in Okinawa.

Kendō, a kind of fencing, was born from the martial arts of warriors. *Shinai*, or bamboo sword, together with *men* (face mask) and *dō-ate* (body protector) began being used in the Edo period (1600–1868).

Kyūdō, or Japanese archery, acquired its name in the 20th century, although its origin dates back to ancient times. Two different kinds of shooting ranges, a shorter one in which competitors shoot at a target while sitting, and a longer one in which competitors shoot standing, are used in *kyūdō* matches.

One commonality of sports derived from Japanese martial arts is that they emphasize courtesy and mental discipline.

• How many professional baseball teams are there in Japan?

There are 12 teams in total, 6 in the Central League and 6 in the Pacific League.

The 12 teams have their farm teams, which comprise the Eastern League and the Western League.

Baseball was introduced from the United States to Japan in 1931, and the "Dai-Nihon Tōkyō Yakyū Club," the original name of the present Yomiuri Giants, was founded in 1934. The Japan Professional Baseball League was launched in 1936

ムで，全日本職業野球連盟が発足しました。現在の2リーグ制になったのは，1949年からです。

1995年，野茂英雄が華々しくアメリカの大リーグに登場し，1年目に大成功したことにより，日本のプロ野球も注目を集めました。

Q: プロサッカーはどんな状況ですか？

日本のプロのサッカーのリーグをJリーグと言います。Japan Professional Football League の愛称です。

1993年に開幕したのですが，この時は，10チームでした。以後，毎年2チームずつが加わって，1996年には16チームになります。

3月から11月までがシーズンで，毎週，水曜日と土曜日を中心に試合が行われています。

日本のサッカーの実力は，最もレベルの高い世界選手権であるワールドカップ・サッカーの予選を，今一息で突破できるところまで来ているのですが，まだ，夢は実現していません。

日常の生活・習慣

Q: 年賀状を平均して1人何通くらい出していますか？

郵政省が発売した1995年用年賀はがきの枚数を単純に人口で割ると35−38枚になるそうです。

外国人の目には，なぜ正月にこんなに沢山の挨拶状を出さなければならないのか，不思議なのだそうですが，クリスマス・カードと同じと思ってもらえばいいでしょう。

with 7 teams in all, and the two-league system was introduced in 1949.

In 1995, Japanese pitcher Nomo Hideo, made his debut in the Major League in the United States and had a successful first year, which created awareness about Japanese professional baseball.

• What is the situation like in professional soccer?

The Japanese professional soccer league is called J. League, which is an abbreviation of the Japan Professional Football League.

Since the league was launched with 10 teams in 1993, 2 teams have been added annually, and in 1996 it will be composed of 16 teams altogether.

The soccer season is from March to November. Games are played on Wednesdays and Saturdays every week during the season.

Having almost qualified for the World Cup Soccer, the most prestigious world soccer championship, the Japanese soccer team continues to strive to realize its dream.

Daily Life in Japan

• On the average, how many New Year's cards does a person send?

Between 35 and 38. That is the number attained by dividing the number of the 1995 New Year's cards the Ministry of Posts and Telecommunications sold by the total population.

Foreign people might wonder why the Japanese send so many cards at New Year's, but those cards are almost like Christmas cards to the Japanese.

New Year's card

日本人にとっては，正月は大事な1年の節目です。その節目の時に，いつもお世話になっている人には，改めてお礼を言い，日ごろご無沙汰している人には，お元気ですかと相手の消息を聞き，こちらの消息を伝えるという，人と人の交流を保つために，日本では大事な習慣になっているのです。

年賀状は12月20日までにポストに投函すると，日本全国どこでも元旦（1月1日）に配達してくれます。

Q: 初詣(はつもうで)でのご利益は何ですか？

The first visit of the year to a shrine

一般には，年の初めに神社で1年の無事と平安を祈願するのが初詣でです。なかでも，松の内と言われる1月7日までに七福神(しちふくじん)（恵比寿(えびす)，大黒天(だいこくてん)，毘沙門天(びしゃもんてん)，弁財天(べんざいてん)，布袋(ほてい)，福禄寿(ふくろくじゅ)，寿老人(じゅろうじん)をそれぞれお祀(まつ)りしている神社）のすべてに詣でると，7種の幸福，つまり，商売繁盛，財運，戦勝運，知恵，徳望，長寿，福徳が得られるとされています

また，受験生やその家族が学問の神様に志望校合格を祈願したり，独身者が縁結びの神様に良縁を祈願するなど，身近で切実なご利益を期待して参拝する人もいます。

Q: お中元，お歳暮は，だれに何のために贈るのですか？

いずれも，日ごろお世話になっている人にお礼として贈ります。恩師，仲人，会社の上司，取引先，習い事の先生，親戚，離れて暮らしている両親，などです。

The New Year holidays are very important for the Japanese as a transition period to a new year. They use this occasion to express gratitude to people who have taken care of them and to send greetings to those they rarely see, informing them of how they are doing. So, it is an important custom for keeping in touch and maintaining friendships.

If cards are mailed by December 20, they will be delivered on January 1st all over Japan.

- **What is the benefit of visiting shrines over the New Year holidays?**

Generally speaking, people visit shrines at the beginning of the year to pray for safety and peace throughout the year. Particularly, it is said that if they visit the shrines of the Seven Lucky Gods (*Ebisu, Daikokuten, Bishamonten, Benzaiten, Hotei, Fukurokuju, Jurōjin*) by January 7 during the period called *Matsunouchi*, they will achieve seven happinesses: i.e., business prosperity, financial gain, victory, wisdom, virtue, longevity, and good luck.

Also, some people pay visits in the hopes of obtaining more direct and necessary benefits like students preparing for entrance examinations and their families, who pray that they pass the exams, or singles who hope to find good partners.

- **To whom and for what reason are summer and winter gifts given?**

Both are gifts to those who have taken care of the sender given to express gratitude to teachers, go-betweens, company supervisors, business clients, tutors, relatives, faraway parents, and others.

お中元はもともと7月15日を指す言葉だったので，7月上旬から15日ごろまでに贈るのが適当です。

お歳暮は，12月上旬から20日頃までに届けます。年に1度のお礼，ということであれば，お歳暮だけでもいいのです。

Q: 正しいおじぎの仕方はどうするのですか？

Bowing

相手と一定の距離をおいて向かい合い，互いに上体を曲げて頭を下げるのが基本です。頭の下げ方は，相手との関係や，その場の状況によって異なります。

女性の場合，手に何も持っていないときには，両手を重ねるように体の前で合わせておじぎをするのが普通です。

椅子に座っているときは，椅子から立ち上がって行います。また，座布団（ざぶとん）を敷いて座っている場合には，座布団から降りて行います。そのとき，体の前で畳や床に軽く両手をつきます。

また，おじぎだけですませないで，その場に応じた挨拶の言葉を交わすことが必要であることは，握手の場合と同じです。

Q: 日本人は握手は嫌いなのですか？

欧米人の到来とともに，この握手という挨拶に日本人は出会ったわけですが，挨拶の仕方に身分の上下でさまざまな格式がある日本では，そう簡単に，異国の人の手を握るわけにはいかなかったでしょう。

しかも，日本の封建社会では，男女が同席をすることも，親しく言葉を交わすこともいけないとされ，まして手を握り合うことなどもってのほ

Chūgen, or summer gifts, literally means July 15, so it is appropriate to send them from around the beginning through mid-July.

Winter gifts should be delivered between early December and the 20th. When expressing gratitude once a year, the winter gift is sufficient.

• What is the correct way of bowing?

The basic way is to lower the head by bending the upper body, standing face to face with the person you're bowing to, leaving a certain distance in between. The degree to which one lowers one's head differs according to the relationship with the person, the situation, etc.

Women usually put their hands one on top of the other in front of the body, and bow in this way if they are not holding anything in their hands.

If they're sitting in a chair, they stand up to bow. If they're sitting on a *zabuton*, or a cushion, they move from it to bow and put both hands lightly on the *tatami* mat or on the floor in front of their body when bowing.

It is also necessary to exchange appropriate greetings when bowing, as well as when shaking hands.

• Do Japanese dislike shaking hands?

The custom of shaking hands came to Japan from the west. At that time, it was not so easy for Japanese to shake hands with foreigners, as they had been accustomed to traditional hierarchical forms of greetings according to class.

Additionally, under the Japanese feudal system, men and women had been prohibited from attending the same function or exchanging greetings in a friendly manner, so shaking

かとされてきましたから，女性とも握手をするなどということが，挨拶としてなじまなかったことは当然です。

現在では，欧米人と接する機会が多いビジネスマンたちは，堂々と握手をするようになりました。しかし，ふだんの生活の中で日本人同士が握手をすることは，まだまだ多いとは言えません。

Q: 挨拶のキスをすることはありますか?

浮世絵の春画(しゅんが)にはよく見られるように，性愛の表現としてのキスは昔からあって，「口吸い」と呼んでいました。性愛の行為としては，民族を問わず，人間としてごく自然な行為なのでしょう。

しかし，挨拶のキスとなると，握手以上に日本人には抵抗があります。テレビで，ロシア人が男性同士でもくちびるを合わせて挨拶をしたりしているのを見ますと，日本人は唖然とします。

様々なキスの習慣については外国映画で見慣れましたから，ほっぺにチュッ，という程度は，日本人も抵抗がなくなっていますが，自分の方から顔を寄せてくる日本人はいないと思ってください。

Q: じゃんけんはどうやるのですか?

Gū

Choki

じゃんけんは，勝ち負けを決めるため用いられます。

普通は片手で行い，拳を握ったグー(石)，手のひらを開いたパー(紙)，人差し指と中指，または親指と人差し指を開いたチョキ(ハサミ)のいずれかを「じゃんけんぽん」という掛け声とともに，相手に見えるように出します。

hands was inconceivable. It was natural, therefore, that shaking hands with women was not easily accepted as a greeting in those days.

At present, Japanese businessmen who have many occasions to meet westerners shake hands comfortably. However, Japanese do not shake hands frequently in daily life.

• Do they kiss when greeting?

As seen in the *shun-ga* (erotic picture), Japanese historically kissed as an expression of sexual love, which was called *kuchisui*, or 'lip sucking.' Kissing is a natural and a universal way of expressing human sexual love.

However, Japanese are reluctant to kiss as a greeting, and prefer to shake hands. For example, a TV scene where Russian men are seen kissing on the lips as a greeting is shocking to them.

Japanese have become more accustomed to various ways of kissing through seeing foreign movies, so they might not be surprised to be kissed lightly on the cheeks as a greeting, but it's unlikely that they would come up to you for a "greeting" kiss.

• How do you play *janken* (scissors, paper, stone)?

Janken is played to determine who wins and who loses.

It is usually played with one hand to make one of the signs at the call "*jan-ken-pon*": *Gū* (stone) is shown with the hand in a fist, *pā* (paper) is shown with the hand open wide, or *choki* (scissors) is shown with the forefinger and middle finger open, or the thumb and forefinger open, while the other fingers are bent.

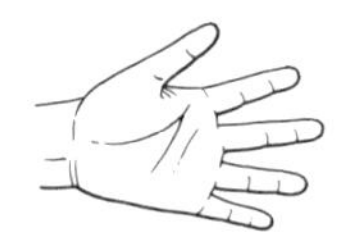
Pā

グーはチョキに，チョキはパーに，パーはグーに勝ちます。皆が同じものを出したりして勝負がつかなかった場合は，「あいこでしょ」と言いながらやり直します。

Q: 日本人の名前には意味があるんですか？

江戸時代まで，姓（苗字）を持つことは武士階級の特権でした。つまり，庶民は弥吉とか，梅とかいう名前だけだったのです。

ところが，明治維新の後，1875年に，全国民は必ず苗字を持つように，という法令が出され，有名な武家や貴族の名前を無断借用したり，漁師だからと魚の名前をつけたりした人もいたといいます。

姓は，地名から由来したものが圧倒的に多いようです。また，職業によってよくみられる姓もあり，例えば，鈴木，小野は神職が多いとされています。大陸から帰化した人たちの姓などもあります。秦（はた），宗（そう）などです。

日本で多い名前のベスト10は，統計によって多少違いますが，佐藤，鈴木，高橋，伊藤，渡辺，斎藤，田中，小林，佐々木，山本で，佐藤さん，鈴木さんは全国で200万人ずつくらいいるそうです。

Q: 日本人はどんな花や植物が好きですか？

こんなデータがあります。1993年に日本で卸売りされた花の本数の概算です。第1位はキクで20億本，第2位はカーネーションで5億9000万本，第3位はバラで4億3000万本，第4位はユリで2億本です。

Gū wins over *choki*; *choki* wins over *pā*, and *pā* wins over *gū*. If the players show the same signs and can't decide who wins, they repeat the motion with the call *aiko-de-sho*, which means "tie."

• What do Japanese names represent?

Until the Edo period (1600–1868), having a surname was a privilege given exclusively to the warrior class. Common people only had a first name such as Yakichi or Ume.

However, in 1875 the Meiji government enacted a law requiring all citizens to have surnames. Some borrowed names of famous warriors or aristocrats, and others used the names of fish because they were fishermen.

A great majority of family names are derived from names of locations. Some names represent occupations. For example, Suzuki and Ono are common for people with ancestors engaged in jobs related to shrines. Hata and Sō are names of people from the Asian continent who were nationalized as Japanese citizens.

The 10 most common Japanese names in descending order are Satō, Suzuki, Takahashi, Itō, Watanabe, Saitō, Tanaka, Kobayashi, Sasaki, and Yamamoto. There are about 2 million Satōs and 2 million Suzukis in Japan.

• What kind of plants are popular with Japanese?

According to a rough calculation of the total number of flowers sold domestically at wholesale in 1993, chrysanthemums were ranked at the top with sales of 2 billion, carnations took second place with 590 million, roses took the third place with 430 million, and lilies came in fourth place with 200 million.

キクの使用量が多いのは，法事などで仏前に捧げる花はキクが主体だからです。カーネーションは，母の日に母親にあげるという習慣があり，このためにも消費量が多いのです

しかし，いろんな層の人たちの好みとしては，バラ，ユリなどを挙げる人が多いようです。

それから，忘れてならない花は桜です。春になると，日本人の多くは，桜の花を求めて野山や公園にくり出します。そして，桜の花の下で宴会を開きます。この「花見」という言葉の花は，何の花と言わないでも，桜の花をさしているくらいです。

Q: 日本人はどんな動物が好きですか？

身近の動物としてなら，やはり，イヌとネコということになるでしょう。日本では，イヌもネコも，およそ400万匹ほどが飼われています。

日本人にはキツネとタヌキもなじみのある動物でした。昔は、変身して人をだますと言われ，たくさんの伝説や昔話に登場しています。

Q: 松，竹，梅，鶴，亀がめでたいと言われる理由は何ですか？

松，竹，梅をめでたいものとする考えは，もともとは中国のものでした。

中国では，冬の厳しい寒さにも負けずに葉の緑を保つ松，竹と，春に他のものに先がけて花を開く梅を，高潔・節操・清純のシンボルとしてとらえたのです。この考え方が日本に入ってきたのは，8世紀の奈良時代だと言われています。

One of the reasons why the consumption of chrysanthemums is so high is that they are often used as offerings before the tablet of the deceased in Buddhist rites. Carnations are popular flowers on Mother's Day.

Many say that roses and lilies are generally liked by people of all walks of life.

When one talks about flowers the Japanese enjoy, one cannot forget cherry blossoms. In spring, people go out to mountains and parks for cherry blossoms, and have a party under cherry trees. Whenever one goes "flower viewing," one does not even need to mention which flower will be viewed.

• What kind of animals are popular in Japan?

As for domesticated animals, dogs and cats are the most common. The number of dogs and cats kept in Japanese households is said to be approximately 4 million each.

In the form of legends and fairy tales, foxes and raccoons have been familiar with the Japanese. In olden times, these animals were believed to trick people by transforming themselves.

• Why do the Japanese believe that pine trees, bamboos, plum trees, cranes, and tortoises are symbols of happiness and good luck?

The idea of cherishing pine trees, bamboos and plum trees as symbols of happiness and good luck originally came from China.

Pine trees and bamboos maintain their green leaves even in the severest cold of winter, and plum blossoms bloom long before spring starts. Therefore, the Chinese regarded them as symbols of nobleness, integrity, and purity. The Japanese imported this idea from China in the Nara period, around the 8th century.

また，鶴は優雅な姿をしていること，亀は寿命が長いことから，おめでたい生き物とされるのです。「鶴は千年，亀は万年」というたとえがあります。

Q: 日本人に人気のある占いは何ですか?

Fortuneteller

昔からあるのは，暦法(れきほう)とおみくじです。暦法は暮らしの行動基準やその日の吉凶などを記したカレンダーの一種，おみくじは神仏に祈願して吉凶を占うくじです。

また，よく話題になるのは星座占いと血液型占いの2つです。特に星座占いは女性に人気です。最近では，東西南北を基準にした方角で占う風水が，ちょっとしたブームになっています。

血液型占いとは，血液型によって人の性格が違うので，そこから人と人との相性や運勢を占う，というものですが，実は日本だけの人気のようです。血液型は遺伝しますが，それが性格を左右するかどうか，医学的にはまったく証明されていません。

Q: 十二支とは何ですか?

時刻や方角を12に分けて，それぞれに動物の名前をあてたものです。すべての時間は12を単位として移り変わるとした古代中国の考えからきており，日本では12年を一回りとして各年に動物をあてたものが一般によく知られています。

Cranes and tortoises are considered blessed animals because the former have graceful figures, and the latter enjoy longevity. There is a saying that goes "Cranes live for thousand years, and tortoises for ten thousand years."

• What form of fortune-telling is popular among the Japanese?

Traditional fortune-telling is done using a special calendar and written oracles. The calendar describes the norms for living and the fortune of the day. Written oracles are fortunes which people draw, praying to the gods or to Buddha for good luck.

Also, two kinds of fortune-telling which have become popular topics of conversation these days are horoscopes and fortune-telling by blood-type. Horoscopes are particularly popular among women. Recently, *feng shui* (wind and water) which tells fortunes based on direction has become very popular.

Fortune-telling by blood-type is based on the assumption that people have different characters according to their blood type. Some blood types harmonize well with others, and bring good luck. This style of fortune-telling seems to be popular only in Japan. Blood-type is inherited, but whether it can help categorize or define people's characters cannot be proved medically.

• What are the twelve zodiac signs?

These are the result of zoning time and direction into twelve blocks, each block being given a name of an animal based on the ancient Chinese concept that all time shifts based on these twelve units. In Japan, zoning of the twelve-year cycle, with a different animal in each zone is fairly common.

12の動物というのは順番に子（ネズミ），丑（牛），寅（虎），卯（兎），辰（竜），巳（蛇），午（馬），未（羊），申（猿），酉（鳥），戌（犬），亥（猪）です。生まれた年の動物によって，その人の性格や運勢が決まると言われています。ちなみに，1996年は子，つまりネズミ年です。

Q:「仏滅」とか「友引」というのは何ですか？

これは『六曜』というものからきており，先勝・友引・先負・仏滅・大安・赤口という6種類の運勢が，毎日順番に現れてくるという，江戸時代からの信仰です。そもそもは中国から来た歴法です。

それぞれに幸運，不運がついていて，例えば仏滅は最悪の日なので，この日に結婚式を行うことは嫌われます。幸運な日とされる大安と比べると，結婚式の数は3分の1くらいになってしまいます。

また友引は良くも悪くもない日ですが，文字通り「友達を引っぱってしまう」というので，この日に葬式をすることは嫌われます。もちろん科学的な根拠はないのですが，この俗信は現代でも根強い力を持っています。

Q:日本人になじみの妖怪にはどんなものがいますか？

愉快な妖怪が多数いますが，代表選手としていくつかを紹介するに止めます。

まず「河童」です。4，5歳の子供ぐらいの大きさで，背中に甲羅があり，頭に水が入った皿があり，手足にひれがあります。水陸両棲です。

「鬼」は身長が2.5m以上もあり，体の色は赤，

The twelve animals are: mouse, cow, tiger, rabbit, dragon, snake, horse, sheep, monkey, bird, dog, and boar, each determining a person's character and destiny who are born in that year. For example, the year 1996 is the year of the mouse.

• What are the days *Butsumetsu* (Buddha's death) or *Tomobiki* (trail day)?

These days originated from *Rokuyō* (six days), a belief from the Edo period (1603–1868) in which six different fortunes appear daily in this order: *Senshō*, *Tomobiki*, *Sempu*, *Butsumetsu*, *Taian*, and *Shakku*. That is a kind of fortune-telling calendar which came from China.

Each fortune has its advantage and disadvantage, but *Butsumetsu* is considered the "worst day," so people hesitate to have weddings on that day. The number of weddings on *Butsumetsu* is about a third of those held on the "good luck" day of *Taian*.

Tomobiki is neither a good nor bad day, but it literally means "pull away friends," so people do not like to have funerals on this day. There is no scientific grounds for these folk beliefs, but they have a deep-rooted support, even today.

• What ghosts or spirits are popular among the Japanese?

There are a lot of comic and mischievous spirits. Here are a few:

The first is a *kappa*, or water sprite, which is as tall as a four-or five-year-old child. It has a shell on its back, a dish with water on top of its head, and fins on its hands and feet. It lives both on land and in water.

Oni, a demon, is taller than 2.5 meters (8.2 feet) and its

青，黒などがあります。頭には2本の角があり，好きな食べ物は人間！

「天狗」は長い鼻を持ち，顔は真っ赤です。山伏（やまぶし）の姿をして高い下駄をはいています。子供をさらって行きます。

「一つ目小僧」は，文字通り顔の真ん中に大きな目が1つ。悪いいたずらはしません。

「海坊主」はぬるぬるした大きい頭を持ち，海の中から顔を出します。船員たちは海坊主を見ても，知らん顔をしなければなりません。そうしないと，船を沈められてしまいます。

「雪女」は，雪の夜に白い着物を着て現れる雪の精です。

日本の妖怪たち
Japanese ghosts or spirits

天狗
Tengu

一つ目小僧
Hitotsume-kozō

鬼
Oni

body is red, blue or black. It has two horns protruding from its head. Its favorite food is the human being!

Tengu, a long-nosed goblin, has a long nose and a very red face. It wears the costume of a *yamabushi*, or a mountain priest, and tall *geta* (wooden clogs). It kidnaps children.

Hitotsume-kozō, a one-eyed goblin, literally has a large eye in the center of his face. It does not play tricks.

Umibōzu, a sea goblin, has a big, slimy head which sticks out from the sea. A ship's crew should ignore it if they find it in the sea. If they do not, it will sink the ship.

Yukionna, a snow woman, is a snow spirit who appears in a white *kimono* on a snowy night.

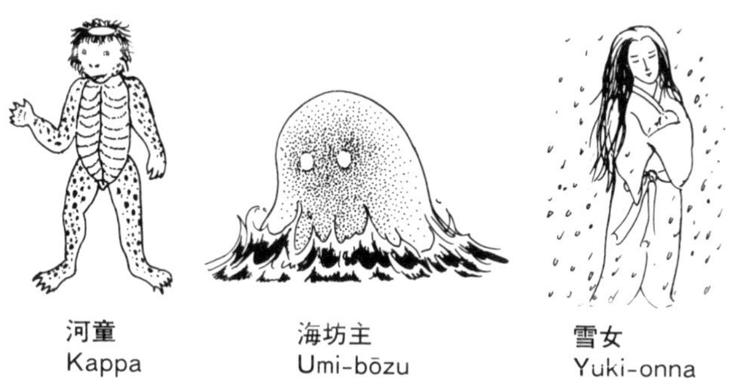

河童
Kappa

海坊主
Umi-bōzu

雪女
Yuki-onna

索引

Index

日本語索引　　Japanese Index

英語索引 English Index

英語で話す「日本」Q&A

Talking About Japan Q&A

1996年4月19日　第1刷発行
1998年6月10日　第19刷発行

編　著　講談社インターナショナル株式会社
　　　　株式会社　翻訳情報センター

発行者　野間佐和子

発行所　講談社インターナショナル株式会社
　　　　〒112-8652　東京都文京区音羽 1-17-14
　　　　電話：03-3944-6493（編集）
　　　　　　　03-3944-6492（営業）

印刷所　大日本印刷株式会社

製本所　株式会社　堅省堂

定価はカバーに表示してあります。

ISBN4-7700-2026-0

英語で読む日本史
Japanese History : 11 Experts Reflect on the Past　KBB 4

英文日本大事典 編　224ページ　ISBN 4-7700-2024-4

11人の超一流ジャパノロジストたちが英語で書き下ろした日本全史。外国人の目から見た日本史はどういうものか、また日本の歴史事項を英語で何と表現するのか。新しい視点が想像力をかき立てます。

日本を創った100人
100 Japanese You Should Know　KBB 25

板坂 元 監修　英文日本大事典 編　240ページ　ISBN4-7700-2159-3

混沌と激動を乗り越え築き上げられた現在の日本。その長い歴史の節目節目で大きな役割を果たした歴史上のキーパーソン100人を、超一流のジャパノロジストたちが解説。グローバルな大競争時代を迎えた今、彼らの生き方が大きな指針となります。

英語で話す「日本の謎」Q＆A　外国人が聞きたがる100のWHY
100 Tough Questions for Japan　KBB 11

板坂　元 監修　240ページ　ISBN 4-7700-2091-0

なぜ、結婚式は教会で、葬式はお寺でなんてことができるの？　なぜ、大人までがマンガを読むの？　なぜ、時間とお金をかけてお茶を飲む練習をするの？――こんな外国人の問いをつきつめてゆくと、日本文化の核心が見えてきます。

英語で話す「日本の心」　和英辞典では引けないキーワード197
Keys to the Japanese Heart and Soul　KBB 12

英文日本大事典 編　328ページ　ISBN 4-7700-2082-1

一流のジャパノロジスト53人が解説した「日本の心」を知るためのキーワード集。「わび」「さび」「義理人情」「甘え」「根回し」「談合」「みそぎ」など、日本人特有な「心の動き」を外国人に説明するための強力なツールです。

英語で話す「日本の文化」
Japan as I See It　KBB 22

NHK国際放送局文化ﾌﾟﾛｼﾞｪｸﾄ 編　ﾀﾞﾝ・ｹﾆｰ 訳　196ページ　ISBN 4-7700-2197-6

金田一春彦、遠藤周作、梅原猛、平川祐弘、西堀栄三郎、鯖田豊之、野村万作、井上靖、小松左京、中根千枝の１０人が、日本文化の「謎」を解く。NHKの国際放送で２１の言語で放送され、分かりやすいと世界中で大好評。

茶の本
The Book of Tea　KBB 28

岡倉天心 著　千 宗室 序と跋　浅野 晃 訳　264ページ　ISBN 4-7700-2379-0

一碗の茶をすする、そのささやかで簡潔な行為の中に、偉大な精神が宿っている――茶道によせて、日本と東洋の精神文化の素晴らしさを明かし、アジアの理想が回復されることを英文で呼びかけた本書は、日本の心を英語で明かす不朽の名著。

ニッポン不思議発見！　日本文化を英語で語る５０の名エッセイ集
Discover Japan: Words, Customs and Concepts KBB 14

日本文化研究所 編　松本道弘 訳　260ページ　ISBN 4-7700-2142-9

絶望的な場合ですら、日本人は「そこをなんとか」という言葉を使って、相手に甘えようとする……こんな指摘をうけると、いかに日本人は独特なものの考え方をしているか分かります。あなたも「不思議」を発見してみませんか。

ニッポン見聞録　大好きな日本人に贈る新･開国論
Heisei Highs and Lows KBB 8

ﾄﾑ・ﾘｰﾄﾞ 著　216ページ　ISBN 4-7700-2092-9

国際化の進む日本ですが、アメリカのジャーナリストが鋭い目と耳で浮き彫りにしたニッポンの姿は、驚くほど平穏でいとおしく、恥ずかしいくらい強欲で無知なものでした。トムが大好きな日本人へ贈る新・開国論。

「Japan」クリッピング　ワシントンポストが書いた「日本」
Views of Japan from The Washington Post Newsroom KBB 6

東郷茂彦 著　256ページ　ISBN 4-7700-2023-6

アメリカの世論をリードするワシントン・ポストに書かれた「Japan」……政治、外交、経済、社会のジャンルで取り上げられた日本の姿を、国際ジャーナリストが解説し、その背後にある問題点を浮き彫りにする一冊。

NHK「ニュースのキーワード」
NHK: Key Words in the News KBB 26

NHK国際放送局　「ﾆｭｰｽのｷｰﾜｰﾄﾞ」 ﾌﾟﾛｼﾞｪｸﾄ 編　232ページ　ISBN4-7700-2342-1

日本で話題になっている時事問題を解説する、NHK国際放送の番組「ニュースのキーワード」から「総会屋」「日本版ビッグバン」「ダイオキシン」など、33のキーワードを収録しました。国際的観点からの解説が、現代の日本の姿を浮き彫りにします。

ベスト・オブ・天声人語
VOX POPULI, VOX DEI KBB 23

朝日新聞論説委員室 著　朝日ｲﾌﾞﾆﾝｸﾞﾆｭｰｽ 訳　280ページ　ISBN4-7700-2166-6

「天声人語」は「朝日新聞」の名コラムというよりも、日本を代表するコラムです。香港返還、アムラー現象、たまごっち、マザー・テレサの死など、現代を読み解く傑作56編を、社会・世相、政治、スポーツなどのジャンル別に収録しました。

誤解される日本人　外国人がとまどう４１の疑問
The Inscrutable Japanese KBB 20

ﾒﾘﾃﾞｨｱﾝ・ﾘｿｰｼｽ・ｱｿｼｴｲﾂ 編　賀川　洋 著　224ページ　ISBN 4-7700-2129-1

あなたのちょっとした仕草や表情が大きな誤解を招いているかもしれません。「日本人はどんなときに誤解を受けるのか？」そのメカニズムを解説し、「どのように外国人に説明すればよいか」最善の解決策を披露します。

ビジュアル 英語で読む日本国憲法
The Constitution of Japan

KBB 18

英文日本大百科事典　編　　208ページ　ISBN 4-7700-2191-7

難しいと思っていた「日本国憲法」も、英語で読むと不思議とよく分かります。日本国憲法を、59点の写真を使って、バイリンガルで分かりやすく解説しました。条文中に出てくる難解な日本語には、ルビや説明が付いています。

イラスト 日本まるごと事典
Japan at a Glance

KBB 17

インターナショナル・インターンシップ・プログラムス 著　　248ページ（2色刷）　ISBN 4-7700-2080-5

1000点以上のイラストを使って日本のすべてを紹介――自然、文化、社会はもちろんのこと、折り紙の折り方、着物の着方から、ナベで米を炊く方法や「あっちむいてホイ」の遊び方まで国際交流に必要な知識とノウハウを満載。

英語で折り紙
Origami in English

KBB 3

山口　真 著　　160ページ　ISBN 4-7700-2027-9

たった一枚の紙から無数の造形が生まれ出る‥‥外国の人たちは、その面白さに目を見張ります。折るとき、英語で説明できるようにバイリンガルにしました。ホームステイ、留学、海外駐在に必携の一冊です。

英語で日本料理
100 Recipes from Japanese Cooking

KBB 15

辻調理師専門学校　畑耕一郎, 近藤一樹 著
268ページ（カラー口絵16ページ）　ISBN 4-7700-2079-1

外国の人と親しくなる最高の手段は、日本料理を作ってあげること、そしてその作り方を教えてあげることです。代表的な日本料理100品の作り方を、外国の計量法も入れながら、バイリンガルで分かりやすく解説しました。

ドタンバのマナー
The Ultimate Guide to Etiquette in Japan

KBB 27

サトウサンペイ 著　　240ページ（オールカラー）　ISBN 4-7700-2193-3

サンペイ流家元が自らしでかした「日常のヘマ」「海外でのヘマ」を一目で分かるようにマンガにした、フレッシュマンに贈る究極のマナー集。新社会人必読！知っていればすむことなのに、知らないために嫌われたり、憎まれてはかないません。

アメリカ日常生活のマナーQ&A
Do As Americans Do

KBB 13

ジェームス・M・バーダマン, 倫子・バーダマン 著　　256ページ　ISBN 4-7700-2128-3

"How do you do?" に "How do you do?" と答えてはいけないということ、ご存知でしたか？　日本では当たり前と思われていたことがマナー違反だったのです。旅行で、駐在で、留学でアメリカに行く人必携のマナー集。

日米比較 冠婚葬祭のマナー
Do It Right : Japanese & American Social Etiquette KBB 2

ジェームス・M・バーダマン, 倫子・バーダマン 著 184ページ ISBN 4-7700-2025-2

アメリカでは結婚式や葬式はどのように行われるのか？　お祝いや香典は？……そしてアメリカの人たちも、日本の事情を知りたがります。これだけあればもう困らない。日米冠婚葬祭マニュアル、バイリンガル版。

英語で話す「仏教」Q&A
Talking About Buddhism Q & A KBB 24

高田佳人 著　ジェームス・M・バーダマン 訳 240ページ ISBN4-7700-2161-5

四十九日までに7回も法事をするのは、「亡くなった人が7回受ける裁判をこの世から応援するため」だということ、ご存じでしたか？　これだけは知っておきたい「仏教」に関することがらを、やさしい英語で説明できるようにした入門書です。

まんが 日本昔ばなし
Once Upon a Time in Japan KBB 16

川内彩友美 編　ラルフ・マッカーシー 訳 160ページ ISBN 4-7700-2173-9

人気テレビシリーズ「まんが日本昔ばなし」から、「桃太郎」「金太郎」「一寸法師」など、より抜きの名作8話をラルフ・マッカーシーの名訳でお届けします。ホームステイなどでも役に立つ一冊です。

ベスト・オブ 宮沢賢治短編集
The Tales of Miyazawa Kenji KBB 5

宮沢賢治 著　ジョン・ベスター 訳 208ページ ISBN 4-7700-2081-3

「注文の多い料理店」「どんぐりと山猫」「祭の晩」「鹿踊りのはじまり」「土神ときつね」「オツベルと象」「毒もみの好きな署長さん」「セロ弾きのゴーシュ」の代表作8編を精選。ジョン・ベスターの名訳でどうぞ。

銀河鉄道の夜
Night Train to the Stars KBB 10

宮沢賢治 著　ジョン・ベスター 訳 176ページ ISBN 4-7700-2131-3

賢治童話の中でも最も人気の高い「銀河鉄道の夜」は、賢治の宗教心と科学精神が反映された独特の世界――天空、自然、大地がみごとに描かれ、光と音と動きに満ち溢れています。ジョバンニと一緒に銀河を旅してみませんか。

ベスト・オブ 窓ぎわのトットちゃん
Best of Totto-chan : The Little Girl at the Window KBB 9

黒柳徹子 著　ドロシー・ブリトン 訳 232ページ ISBN 4-7700-2127-5

小学校一年生にして「退学」になったトットちゃんは、転校先の校長先生に「君は本当はいい子なんだよ」と温かい言葉のシャワーで励まされます…バイリンガル版で、あの空前の大ベストセラーの感動をもう一度！

マザー・グース　愛される唄70選
Mother Goose : 70 Nursery Rhymes　KBB 7

谷川俊太郎 訳　渡辺　茂 解説　176ページ　ISBN 4-7700-2078-3

「マイ・フェア・レディー」や「お熱いのがお好き」という題名も、マザー・グースからの引用だったってこと、ご存じでしたか？ 英米人にとって必須教養であるこの童謡集を、詩人・谷川俊太郎の名訳と共にお楽しみください。

ビジネスマン必携！

対訳 英語で話す日本経済Q&A
A Bilingual Guide to the Japanese Economy

NHK国際放送局経済プロジェクト・
大和総研経済調査部 編

46判（128 x 188 mm）仮製　368ページ

ISBN 4-7700-1942-4

NHK国際放送で好評を得た番組が本になりました。クイズと会話形式で楽しく読んでいくうちに、日本経済の仕組が分かり、同時に英語にも強くなっていきます。日本語と英語の対応がひと目で分かる編集上の工夫もいっぱい。

わが家の味を海外に

バイリンガル とってもかんたんマイレシピ
Stone Soup : Easy Japanese Home Cooking

渡辺節子 著

B5判変型（189 x 257 mm）　仮製　256ページ

ISBN 4-7700-2061-9

手軽な日本の家庭料理、わが家の味160品目の作り方を英語と日本語で紹介したクッキングブック。作り方や調理器具などのイラストつき、カロリー計算、調理時間もひと目で分かります。

英語と日本語で楽しむ

対訳 サザエさん（全12巻）

The Wonderful World of Sazae-san

長谷川町子［著］　ジェールス・ヤング［訳］

- 吹き出しの中にオリジナルの暖かい雰囲気を大切にした英語、コマの横に日本語が付く対訳形式。
- お正月、こいのぼり、忘年会など日本独特の文化や習慣には、欄外に英語の解説つき。

46判変型（113 x 188 mm）　仮製

第1巻　170ページ　ISBN 4-7700-2075-9
第2巻　168ページ　ISBN 4-7700-2093-7
第3巻　198ページ　ISBN 4-7700-2094-5
第4巻　164ページ　ISBN 4-7700-2149-6
第5巻　176ページ　ISBN 4-7700-2150-X
第6巻　160ページ　ISBN 4-7700-2151-8
第7巻　168ページ　ISBN 4-7700-2152-6
第8巻　168ページ　ISBN 4-7700-2153-4
第9巻　172ページ　ISBN 4-7700-2154-2
第10巻　172ページ　ISBN 4-7700-2155-0
第11巻　176ページ　ISBN 4-7700-2156-9
第12巻　168ページ　ISBN 4-7700-2157-7